Atma

A Romance

Caroline Augusta Frazer

TABLE OF CONTENTS

CHAPTER I.

CHAPTER II.

CHAPTER III.

CHAPTER IV.

CHAPTER V.

CHAPTER VI.

CHAPTER VII.

CHAPTER VIII.

CHAPTER IX.

CHAPTER X.

CHAPTER XI.

CHAPTER XII.

CHAPTER XIII.

CHAPTER XIV.

CHAPTER XV.

CHAPTER XVI.

CHAPTER XVII.

CHAPTER XVIII.

CHAPTER XIX.

CHAPTER XX.

Caroline Augusta Frazer

CHAPTER I.

O that Decay were always beautiful!
How soft the exit of the dying day,
The dying season too, its disarray
Is gold and scarlet, hues of gay misrule,
So it in festive cheer may pass away;
Fading is excellent in earth or air,
With it no budding April may compare,
Nor fragrant June with long love-laden hours;
Sweet is decadence in the quiet bowers
Where summer songs and mirth are fallen asleep,
And sweet the woe when fading violets weep.
O that among things dearer in their wane
Our fallen faiths might numbered be, that so
Religions cherished in their hour of woe
Might linger round the god-deserted fane,
And worshippers be loath to leave and pray
That old-time power return, until there may
Issue a virtue, and the faith revive
And holiness be there, and all the sphere
Be filled with happy altars where shall thrive
The mystic plants of faith and hope to bear
Immortal fruitage of sweet charity;
For I believe that every piety,
And every thirst for truth is gift divine,
The gifts of God are not to me unclean
Though strangely honoured at an unknown shrine.
In temples of the past my spirit fain
For old-time strength and vigour would implore
As in a ruined abbey, fairer for

"The unimaginable touch of time"
We long for the sincerity of yore.
But this is not man's mood, in his regime
Sweet "calm decay" becomes mischance unmeet,
And dying creeds sink to extinction,
Hooted, and scorned, and sepultured in hate,
Denied their rosary of good deeds and boon
Of reverence and holy unction—
First in the list of crimes man writes defeat.
These purest dreams of this our low estate,
White-robed vestals, fond and vain designs,
I lay a wreath at your forgotten shrines.

Nearly four hundred years ago, Nanak, a man of a gentle spirit, lived in the Punjaub, and taught that God is a spirit. He enunciated the solemn truth that no soul shall find God until it be first found of Him. This is true religion. The soul that apprehends it readjusts its affairs, looks unto God, and quietly waits for Him. The existence of an Omnipresent Holiness was alike the beginning and the burden of his theology, and in the light of that truth all the earth became holy to him. His followers abjured idolatry and sought to know only the invisible things of the spirit. He did not seek to establish a church; the truths which he knew, in their essence discountenance a visible semblance of divine authority, and Nanak simply spoke them to him who would hear,—emperor or beggar,—until in 1540 he went into that spiritual world, which even here had been for him the real one.

And then an oft-told story was repeated; a band of followers elected a successor, laws were necessary as their number increased, and a choice of particular assembling places became expedient. And as

"the trees
That whisper round a temple become soon

Dear as the temple's self,"

so the laws passed into dogmas having equal weight with the truths that Nanak had delivered, and the places became sacred.

Nanak's successors were ten, fulfilling a prophecy which thus limited their number. The compilation of their sayings and doings to form a book which as years went on was venerated more and more, and the founding of Amritsar, chief of their holy places, were the principal things that transpired in the history of the Khalsa during a century and a half, save that the brotherhood was greatly strengthened by Muslim persecution, occurring at intervals.

But with the death of the ninth Guru, by Muslim violence, and the accession of his son Govind, the worldly fortunes of the Khalsa changed. Under the leadership of Govind, a young man of genius and enthusiasm, who comes before us in the two-fold character of religionist and military hero, the Sikhs moved on to a national greatness not dreamed of by Nanak. Govind, who bestowed on himself and his followers the title of Singh, or lion-hearted, hitherto an epithet appropriated in this connection by the Rajpoot nobility, devoted the strong energies of his vigourous and daring nature to the purpose of establishing the faith of Nanak by force of arms. To this end he constituted the sword a religious symbol, and instituted a sort of worship of steel. The Khalsa became an aggressive force bent on the salvation of surrounding nations by violence, and succeeded so well, that, eighty-five years after Govind's death, the Sikhs, still retaining their character of a religious fellowship, were consolidated into a powerful nation under Ranjit Singh. The dream of her tenth and last Guru was realized, the Khalsa was at her height of worldly prosperity, but her life was no longer the spirit life which had been revealed to her first founder.

And so under Asiatic skies as well as amid European civilization, man laboured to redeem the world, making frantic war on the lying creeds of past ages and proclaiming the merits of his latest discovery.

It is a strange development of human nature this animosity to creeds no longer our own. Why, if I suffer the loss of faith and hope, must I hasten to introduce my brother to my sad plight? I may do so, and perhaps enjoy good conscience in the act by vaunting that I shed light on his spiritual vision. God help my brother if his light be from me. And God help me also, if I have attained so high rank among the blessed before I have learned that the human soul is beyond human aid; that in its eternal relations each soul travels in an orbit of its own and holds correspondence only with its Sun.

CHAPTER II.

A century and a half after, Govind Singh had kindled the hearts of his countrymen with his prophetic visions of a military church regnant on the hills of Kashmir, there took place the struggle which we call the second Sikh war, culminating on the twenty-first of February in the Battle of Gugerat followed by the surrender of the Sikhs to the British under Lord Gough and the disbandment of the Sikh army. And, lo, the Khalsa was as a tale that is told, its clang and clash of warlike achievements a thing that could be no more, its Holy War transformed by failure into a foolish chimera, and the only thing that lived was a memory lingering in quiet souls of the truths that Nanak taught.

"For shapes that come, not at an earthly call,
Will not depart when mortal voices bid."

But many whose faith was in their religion rather than in God felt their spirit falter, and believed that the universe grew dark. This is ever the weakness of disciples, and thus it is that while many flocking to the new standard see all things made plain, others whose hopes are entwined about the displaced creeds suffer an eclipse of faith.

Among those who in the fall of the Khalsa suffered life's last and sorest loss was Raee Singh, an aged man, in whose veins ran the blood of the gentle Nanak. On that March morning when the disbanded army went to lay down their arms before a victorious foe, he descended the mountain slope very slowly. The rest walked in bands of five, of ten, of twenty, but Raee Singh walked alone. Although his flowing beard was white, he did not bear himself erect in the dignity of years; his eyes were fixed on the ground, for the shadow of defeat and dishonour which rested on him was hard to bear.

Presently he stood before the tent of the British general. A great heap of weapons lay there glittering in the sun. As he looked, the pile grew larger, for each Sikh cast his sword there. Raee also extended his arm, grasping his tulwar, but he did not let it go until an officer touched his shoulder and spoke. The blade fell then with a clang, and he turned away. He passed from the camp without seeing it, and took his homeward way as silently as he had come. The dreams of youth make the habit of age, and Raee had revered the Khalsa in childhood, and in manhood he had urged its high commission to his own hurt. As a Khivan proverb has it, "That which goes in with the milk only goes out with the soul," and the soul of Raee Singh gathered the fragments of its broken faith and prepared to depart with them to the Land of Restoration.

He lay for four days, taking no food, and only wetting his lips with the water which his sole surviving son proffered from time to time. His heart was crushed, he was full of years, his end was near; and his son, knowing this, was dumb with sorrow. On the evening of the fourth day he turned his face to the boy, and spoke,

"Son, well beloved,
My parting hour is nigh;
A heavenly peace should glorify
A life approved
By God, by man, by mine own soul;
The record of my stainless years unroll—
My years beset
From infancy to age with pitfalls deep
In pathway winding aye on mountain steep
Of perilous obedience, and yet
In bitterness of soul I lay me down,
Of home bereft, with hope and creed o'erthrown
In woe that will not weep;

Atmâ

My reeling spirit ere from sense set free
Is loosed from mooring, beaten to and fro,
And in the throbbing, quick'ning flesh I know
The lone desertion of the Shoreless Sea.
O Brotherhood!
O hope so high, so fair,
That would the wreck of this sad world repair
Had ye but stood!
Can God forget?
This Khalsa of his own supreme decree
Vanquished, debased, in loss of liberty
Has lost its own mysterious entity.
And yet, and yet,
A strange persuasion fills my breast that He
Who wrecked my home,
Who bade my people from their mountains flee
And friendless roam,
Will soon with tenderest pity welcome me,
And, if my lips be dumb,
Will frame the prayer that fills my dying breast,
And give my heavy-laden spirit rest,
And grant me what He will—His will is best.
I go—I know not where,
Upward or down, or toward the setting sun
None knows,—some shadowy goal is won,
Some unseen issue near,
So oft with death I journeyed hand in hand,
The spectral pageant of his border land
I do not fear.
Weep not when I have passed, but go thy way,
Thou art not portionless nor service free,

A warrior Sikh, for thee a high behest
Abides, to claim thy true-sword's ministry.
Go, Atmâ, from those echoing hillsides, lest
The haunting voices of the vanished say
'Vain is thy travail, poor thine utmost store,
We loved and laboured, lo, we are no more,'
And thy fond heart in fealty to our clay
Fail in allegiance to the name we bore.
Go, seek thy kinsman, to a brother's hand
I gave possession of a gem more fair,
More costly far than gold, than rubies rare,
Thy part and heritage, of him demand
Its just bestowal, and with dauntless tread
Pursue the pathway of thy holy dead."

When the old Sikh had ceased speaking, he lay greatly exhausted. The night deepened. It was a remote spot. Now and then the sound of trampling feet or the tread of a horse climbing the difficult road reached the ear. The hours were long and dreary, but they passed. Morning dawned, and Atmâ found himself alone. He had known that it would be so, and yet it came with the sharpness of an unexpected blow. He mourned, and, as is the way with mourners, he accused himself from hour to hour of having failed in duty to the departed during his lifetime. Looking on the face of the dead, he wondered much where the spirit that so lately had seemed to be with the frame but a single identity, one and indivisible, had fled. He recalled his father's words,

"Upward or down, or toward the setting sun,
None knows,"

and with the recollection, the sense of loss deepened. An old cry rose to his lips, "Oh, that I knew where I might find him!"

The words by which his father had sought to comfort him still sounded in his hearing, but Grief is stronger than Wisdom. Human speech is the least potent of forces, and arguments that clash and clang bravely in the tournament of words, slaying shadows, and planting the flag of triumph over fallen fancies, on entering the lists to combat the fact of Death, but beat the air, and their lusty prowess only fetches a laugh from out of the silence.

CHAPTER III.

After his father's death Atmâ betook himself to Lahore, where dwelt Lehna Singh, only brother of the departed Sikh. A man of a totally different cast of mind, he had early adopted a commercial life, and now, in the enjoyment of a vast fortune, yet undiminished by the contingencies of war, lived in luxury and opulence, his dwelling thronged by Sikhs whose possessions, unlike his own, had melted away in the national catastrophe. The fact of his house being the rendezvous of a discontented faction did not escape British vigilance, the more so as Lehna Singh was one of the eight sirdars appointed to sit in council with the British Resident. But the confidence of his countrymen in him remained unshaken by the appearance among them of British envoys in military state, bearing despatches to the friend of the national foe, and the questionable attitude of Lehna became to the Resident daily more and more the subject of suspicious surmisings.

Indeed, a whisper was afloat of secret messages from Feragpore, whither, before the war, had been removed the Ranee Junda Kovr, deposed Queen of the Punjaub, as a consequence of a detected plot against the life of the Resident, which, together with her sullied reputation,—for she had many lovers,—had induced the council to pronounce her an unfit guardian for the little Maharajah, her son. This clever woman, a constant source of vexation to the Resident, had long forfeited the respect of friend and foe; but her intrepidity, cunning, and unscrupulous thirst for power conspired to render her formidable to the one, and to the other a partisan to be courted and retained. Her messages of insolent defiance to the Durbar are historic, but of the countless schemes and intrigues in which she continued to play the part of chief conspirator we have only heard a portion. Suffice it to say that the faithlessness of her policy alike towards adversary, or ally, and the scandal of her retinue of lovers, had gained for her an ill-repute, that combined with the watch set upon her movements by the British to render men chary of dealings with the little court at Feragpore, where she held mimic state.

But of all these tales of craft and crime Atmâ knew nothing. To him all men were valiant and all women fair and good, and the wife and child of Ranjit Singh, the Lion of the Punjaub, were invested in his fond imaginings with ideal excellence. "To the pure all things are pure," or, as a later genius has voiced it, "He who has been once good is forever great," and Atmâ lived in the corrupt atmosphere of his uncle's house, and took no hurt; nay, his spiritual life by its own dynamic force grew and thrived, for, governed by other laws than those that control our physical natures, the food of the soul is what it desires it to be, and moral poison has often served for nutriment. It is death to souls that desire death. In another sense than Bonaparte's, every man born unto the world may say, "I make circumstances."

And the spacious abode of Lehna Singh had loveliness enough to veil the sordid character of the life that was lived within its walls. Atmâ had not been ignorant of his kinsman's wealth and importance; but it is one thing to hear of wealth and to ponder in critical mood the fleeting nature of this world's weal, and quite another to gaze with the eye on the marvellous results of human thrift. He wandered through lofty and spacious apartments, whose marble arches seemed ever to reveal a fairer scene than had yet met his view. A mimic rivulet ran from room to room in an alabaster channel, and the spray of perfumed fountains cooled the air. Flowers bloomed, leafy vines trailed over priceless screens, and countless mirrors repeated the joyous beauty of the place. He beheld with admiration the gilded and fretted walls and stately domes, the new delights of a palace charmed every sense, and, appealing to poetic fancy, awoke a rapture whose fervency was due less to the entrancement of his present life than to the contemplative habit of one who had first known harmony whilst gazing on the stars, and awaked to the consciousness of beauty among the eternal hills. The ripple of the streamlet in these palace halls revived a half-forgotten music of the heart that had once responded to the gurgle of a brook.

"Heard melodies are sweet, but those unheard are sweeter."

The sympathies that had once been in unison with the rustling thicket stirred into more definite life when an artificial breeze swept by and stirred the heavy foliage of rare plants. He had caught in other days notes of Nature's vast melody. Stray notes were here made to beat to a smaller measure. Thus Art interprets Nature. It was not The Song, but a light and pleasant carol, which pleased the sense of many, and to the ear of the few brought a haunting pain of which they did not know the meaning. Such a one only sighed and said:

"In a former birth I was great and good, and my life was sublime. The ghost of its memory has touched me."

O melody divine, of fantasy
And frenzied mem'ry wrought, advance
From out the shades; O spectral utterance,
Untwine thy chains, thy fair autocracy
Unveil, have being, declare
Thy state and tuneful sovereignty.
Ye gifted ears,
To whom this burdened, sad creation
Sings, now in tones of exultation
Abruptly broken,
Anon in direst lamentation
Obscurely spoken,
Possess your souls in hope, the time

Is coming when th' harmonic chime
Of circling spheres in chant sublime
Will lead the music of the seas,
And call the echoes of the breeze
To one triumphal lay
Whose harmony, whose heavenly harmony
Sounding for aye
In loud and solemn benedicite,
Voices the glory of the Central Day,
And through th' illimitable realms of air
Is borne afar
In wafted echoes that the strain prolong
Through boundless space, and countless worlds among,
Meas'ring the pulsing of each lonely star,
And sounding ceaselessly from sphere to sphere
That note of immortality
That whispers in the sorrow of the sea,
And in the sunrise, and the noonday's rest,
And triumphs in the wild wind's meek surcease,
And in the sad soul's yearning unexpressed,
And unexpressive for perpetual peace.

But the loveliest of Lehna Singh's possessions was Moti, his daughter and only child, the fame of whose beauty had even reached Atmâ in his mountain home. Of her he had dreamt through boyhood's years, and a happy consciousness of her proximity foreshadowed the enchanted hour when he was to behold her and own that his fondest fancies were to her loveliness as darkness to noonday. Her name he had heard whispered in the gay throng of her father's guests, on the memorable first evening of his arrival there; but, strange to tell, next day, when these first hours in a palace seemed to his excited imagination a dream in which mingled in wildest confusion the glitter of diamonds, the perfume of a thousand flowers, the revel of dazzling colors, the bewildering music of unknown instruments, and the intoxication of wonder and bliss, there rang through all only one articulate voice, sounding as if from some leafy ambush amid vague laughter and murmurs of speech, saying:

"But I tell you that Rajah Lal Singh means to pluck the rose of Lehna Singh's garden!"

Caroline Augusta Frazer

CHAPTER IV.

Atmâ loved to wander apart. One day he penetrated to a secluded court, whose beauty and silence charmed him more than anything he had hitherto seen. It was Moti's garden.
"High in air the fountain flung
Its living gems, on sunbeams strung
They wreathed and shook the mists among;
A thousand roses audience held,
For floral state the place was meet,
With blissful light and joy replete,
And depths of sweetness unrevealed.
Glittered and sparkled the revelling spray,
Swelled and receded its silvery lay,
Rustled the roses in fervid array,
In fragrance declaring their costly acclaim,
Wafting on soft winds the redolent fame
Of fantasy, fountain, and tuneful refrain.
Joy, Happiness, and Bliss had here
Alighted when from Eden driven,
Poor wanderers of far other sphere
They languished for their native heaven;
And lingering they glamoured all the place,
The flowers bloomed in airs of Paradise,
That lulled the days to dreams of changeless peace.
No marvel were it if to mortal eyes
This garden seemed the threshold of the skies.
But fountain and roses and glittering spray,
Ambrosial converse and redolent lay
Saddened and dimmed in the radiant day,
Unbroken the yellow sunbeams streamed,

As ever the flashing jewels gleamed.
But a shadow fell
And a silent spell
In homage of one who was fairer than they.
And who was the despot whose wondrous array
Of tyrant charms thus over-wrought
With hues of soft humility
The joys of this enchanting spot?
There stood she, envied of the closing day,
Loved by the evening star,
Moti, than costliest jewel of Cathay
More rare and lovelier far.
Weep balmy tears,
O dear white Rose, and tell to am'rous airs
They waste their sweetness on thy charms, and chide
Their ling'ring dalliance, o'er the whole world wide
Bid them on buoyant morning wings to move,
And whisper "Love;"
Fair winds, be tender of her blissful name,
On soft Æolian strings weave dainty dream,
Let but the dove
Hear a faint echo of her happy name;
But tell her worth,
Say that at sight of her the evening dies
Upon the earth,
And bees and little flower bells still their mirth
And jasmines whisp'ring of her starry eyes.
nd Atmâ spoke, with love and wonder bold,
"Tread I the valley where the fadeless vine
Drops dew immortal and sweet spices grow
From fragrant roots which in that blessed mould,

Atmâ

Watered by tears of penitential woe,
Drank deep of primal peace and balm divine,
When in the morn of time the tale was told
Of forfeit happiness and ruined shrine?
Tell me, O beauteous Spirit of the bower,
Is it thy gentle task when others sleep,
To guard all that a fallen world may keep
Of pristine bliss and lost felicities,
The fragrant memory of a purer hour,
The healing aroma of Paradise?"
Sweet then the blushing maid replied,
"Among the roses I abide,
I wake the bird, I watch the bee,
No greater toil is set for me;
But tell me, pray thee, with what charge indued
You wander in this quiet solitude."
And Atmâ spoke with joyful fervency,
"I hither came on embassy unguessed,
Most blissful vision of my raptured view,
The dusk delights of quietness and rest
Desired I, nor thought to bid adieu
To all content my fond heart ever knew.
Descending angels of my wisest dreams,
Ye kindly genii, bending from above,
Say, in th'allotment of my life's high themes,
Were hours left for love?
A great design and just my soul employs,
Can high resolve and trancéd rest agree?
Or is there aught than loss in changeful joys
Of mortal love, most mortal in its wane
Which I shall see

And call aloud, 'O Love,' in vain, in vain."
"Bloomy roses die,
Sunbeams have no morrow,
Sweetest songs give place to sigh,
Ah, the speechless sorrow,
Pain of by-and-bye.
I too well have known
Gladness lives a-dying,
Joys are often prized when flown,
Loved when past replying,
Sought when left alone.
Sad when roses pine,
Ah, but love is dearer,
Who would dare to quaff this wine
Knowing Fate the bearer,
Guileful fate of mine?
Moti, peerless flower,
Queen of love and gladness,
Tell me in this happy hour,
Will Joy turn to sadness,
And Love's death-night lower?"
Moti, wise as lovely, pondered,
"'Mong the sunbeams I have wandered,
With the flowers friendship made;
Sweetest blossoms wither,
But alike they fade,
Roses die together,
Beauteous death is made.
Comrades e'en in death are flowers,
Always sweet are friendship's bowers.
Lightly sorrow touches twain,

Only solitude is pain."
Mild were the utterings of the cooing dove,
Who did approve
In myrtle ambuscade this tender lore;
The constant plashing of the fountain spray
Melted in easy numbers, dying away
A quiet cadence, while for evermore
Faded the eve in richest livery wove
Of Tyrian dyes and amber woof t'allure
The soft salaam of slowly sinking day.
Stars shone, and Atmâ said, "'Tis well to be,
The things of earth are painted pleasantly."
But pleasantness is light and versatile,
And moods must change and tranquil breezes veer,
And o'er this blissful hour there came a chill
And sullen shadows slowly creeping near
In lengthening lines, and murkier dusk took form
Of all things ominous, disastrous, ill,
And as a mid-day gloom portending storm,
A lowering fate made prophecy of fear,
And Atmâ knew the menace in the air,
As ghostly shudderings of our fearful life
Foretell the advent of th' assassin's knife.
Low sank his heart before the augury
(For life was dearer on this eventide
Than e'er before), and all dismayed, he cried,
"These are the heralds of calamity
That bid me hence, for all too well I know
The pensive pageantry of mortal woe;
O Love, my Love, this sweetest love may flee
But ever grief has cruel constancy,

Late I bode me with dull-shrouded sorrow,
And well I know her doleful voice again.
Hark! the breezes from the nightshade borrow
A heavy burden of lament and pain,
And where Delight held lately sweet hey-day,
Now like spectres pallid moonbeams play,
Very still the little rosebud sleeps,
Heavily the drooping myrrh tree weeps
Sluggish tears upon the darksome mould."
Quick then did Moti speak, by love made bold,
"No cause is there, O Love, for sad affright,
For I have read the portents of the night;
Of envy dies the glowworm when the moon
Is worshipped in the welkin, and the boon
Of costly tears
Dropped by the bleeding tree, to mortal cares
Is healing balm;
The rosebuds dream, Love, and the soft wind's sigh
Is lullaby.
And yet I know that sorry things befal
Sometimes, withal,
For once it was my grievous task to mourn
A turtle dove sore wounded by a thorn."
"O sweetest Dove,
May grief be far from thee,
Who lovest sorrow when thou lovest me;
But changeful love
May yet be fixed by grief no more to rove,
And we by woe be bound in constancy.
O Roses, bear me witness of my truth,
Death with my love were life a thousand-fold,

Dear death were fairer than immortal youth
Could it life's weal in friendly arms enfold.
Dark Angel of the River's brink, draw near,
In stable grasp this sovereign hour assure,
Cast icy glamour o'er my love's sweet cheer,
Forever then shall that dear love endure,
An end of sweets fair Chance may hold in store
Were death of all the changeful moods of time,
And boundless being of my love's sweet prime.
Ah, thorny Roses, prate ye still of ruth
And would me my brief hour of bliss deny?
And yet all happy things to love are sooth,
But I, ah me, this destiny so high
Weighs on my spirit like a drowsy spell,
I cannot joy like those, nor stay, I fail
Before the greatness of my high behest,
Ah, high is holiness, but love is rest,
Yes, love is rest, is rest; then blow, sweet gale
Of soft forgetfulness about me still,
And O, ye Roses, balmy breath exhale
And all my consciousness with slumber fill.
And, O sweet Love, I pray you yield me now
One little pearl from the fair coronal
That crowns the loveliness of that calm brow,
And I, where'er I be, will own its thrall,
And gaze on it and dream until I see
A phantom love, before whom I shall fall
And pray, adoring white-robed purity."

CHAPTER V.

"Your lofty faith and devotion, my son, move me deeply. The heroic spirit of my brother Raee seems once more to incite me to deeds of daring which in these degenerate days would alas be vain."

So spoke Lehna Singh in the midst of luxury and splendour that had been amassed in no hazardous career of adventure or enterprise, but by methods of coldest calculation and avarice. His listeners were his nephew, whom he addressed, and the Rajah Lal Singh, chief favourite of the notorious Ranee, a man of cringing and servile demeanour, notwithstanding his rank, whose crafty smile followed the speaker's words as he scrutinized the countenance of Atmâ, as if to learn their effect. The apartment in which they sat was an inner chamber, small, secluded, and silent, for the fame of Lal, lately Wuzeer to the little Maharajah, but for grave offences disgraced and removed from Lahore, was such as to demand caution on the part of those who would consort with him.

"Before I can explain to you," proceeded Lehna, "the last words of my departed brother, I have a tale to unfold, a tale which will reveal to you in how high a degree your coming has been opportune. In these troubled days a loyal, brave, and trusty friend of the Khalsa is far to seek, and it is in quest of such a one that my honoured guest Rajah Lal Singh has, in the face of much peril, come to me from the Maharanee, now at Feragpore, whither she was sent by Purwunnah, under seal of her infant son, the Maharajah, thus made in tender years the instrument of his mother's disgrace. But on the cruel affronts of our enemies I need not dwell. These things are known to all. The plans which I am about to reveal to you, Atmâ Singh relate to the future, and speak not of disgrace, but of hope; know that in the treasures of Ranjit Singh there was one jewel—a sapphire—of magical property. To its holder it ensured success in war. This jewel, the late Maharajah received from my hands. It was a family heirloom, and descended to your father, the eldest son of our house, through countless generations. Being, when we were both young, in sore straits, and hard pressed for money, he parted with this talisman to me, on condition that after his death I should return it to his eldest surviving son. You may guess the poignancy of the grief with which I tell you then that this heirloom is no longer mine. Many years ago I gave it into the hands of Ranjit Singh for a time, in the belief that its potency would aid our national fortunes" (what equivalent Lehna received, he doubtless deemed it irrelevant to state). "The brilliancy of his career attests its worth. It should have been long ago restored to me, but my efforts to regain it were repeatedly baffled, until I was fain to content myself with the reflection that at least it served the cause, and to trust in the future for its recovery. Believing it to be in the treasury at Lahore, and firmly believing in its potency, those of us who knew of its existence never abandoned hope until its disappearance was, alas! ascertained beyond a doubt. To such, each defeat of the Khalsa caused amazement deeper than consternation. The overthrow of the Sikh power seemed a thing incredible until the recent confiscation and plunder of the treasuries, when it became certain to other vigilant onlookers as well as to myself that the Sapphire of Fate was not in the possession of the true rulers of the Punjaub at the time of their downfall. Contrast the victorious progress of the Lion of the Punjaub with the fallen fortunes of his family, when robbed of what we now believe to be the talisman of his fortunes. Not only does the Ranee believe that the recovery of this gem will ensure the prosperity of the descendants of Ranjit Singh, but I do firmly believe that its re-possession will rally the Sikh forces to form again a conquering faith. Son of Raee, have you the courage to serve the Ranee, to regain this, your inheritance, and in obedience to your father's dying words, to devote it and your own life to a fallen house, whose foes are the foes of the Khalsa?"

Atmâ remained silent during some minutes, plunged in thought, and unconscious of the anxious scrutiny of his companions, who, bending forward, awaited his reply in breathless suspense. It was a shock to know that the heritage which was certainly his had passed from the guardianship of the kinsman to whom it had been entrusted, and indignation mingled with gentler reflections. He had not known the story of the Sapphire, and his thoughts reverted to his father, the meaning of whose reticence on a subject, which must have been full of humiliation and pain, his son sadly divined, and recalling his dying words, indelibly printed on his memory, he felt his high commission to be again renewed and vivified. Perhaps the gentle image of Moti, ever present to fond imagination, dispelled the rising clouds of distrust and resentment, and bade him meet her father's demand with response of like spirit. So now recalling the ingenuous emotion which had glowed in his face during Lehna's tragic account of the recent career of Junda Kowr, he asked where the Sapphire of Fate was to be found.

"At the Court of Golab Singh," replied his uncle, dramatically. "Golab Singh, once a horseman in the employ of Ranjit Singh, now by British machinations usurper of the crown of Kashmir. If you, Atmâ, are a true and faithful adherent of the Khalsa, you will thither repair as an envoy of the Maharanee, and will count her reward lightly won by danger encountered for the faith."

"Inform her highness of my instant readiness to perform her request," replied Atmâ.

Happiness overspread the countenance of Lehna. With a gentle sigh of relief, he abandoned the heroic and magnanimous strain in which his speech had flown, and which to so acute and wary a man of affairs was perhaps unfamiliar. He exchanged a glance of satisfaction with the Rajah, who leaned back among his silken cushions in an attitude of greater comfort than he had allowed to himself during the preceding anxious half-hour.

It only remained to instruct the young Sikh as to the course and manner of his journey, which was to be first to Ferazpore to receive the commands of Junda Kowr, thence to Jummoo, where Golab Singh, the recently appointed ruler of Kashmir, held his brilliant court.

These matters satisfactorily arranged, Rajah Lal with stately ceremony took his leave, and Atmâ found himself alone with his kinsman, who proceeded to matters of not less interest.

"I am honoured," he said, "by your proposed alliance with my house," for Atmâ had disclosed to her father his love for Moti. "I am honoured and deeply moved; but I defer this consummation of my cherished wish until all may know that among many suitors, I chose, to be the husband of my only child, a leal soldier of the Khalsa. But your high nature will, I perceive, count this prize lightly won by peril endured for the Khalsa. You go to-morrow to Ferazpore, where you will meet again Rajah Lal, who has perhaps more influence with our clever Ranee than many a better man. He repairs thither this evening, and will no doubt prepare for you a favourable reception, and you will," he added, laughing, "in all probability be received with the overflowing kindness and unveiled confidence which our British friends deprecate!"

This covert allusion was not understood by the young Sikh, in whose thoughts all men were valiant and all women fair and good. But he experienced a shade of annoyance on learning that he must owe anything to the good offices of Lal Singh. An echo seemed to sound faint and far as in a dream; "Rajah Lal," it seemed to say, "means to pluck the Rose of Lehna Singh's garden."

CHAPTER VI.

A subdued light stole through the latticed windows of the house of Junda Kowr, revealing a court whose hush and shadow contrasted with the busy life that Atmâ had left behind him. The silence and pleasing coolness were in harmonious unison with the gleaming alabaster arches, and the subdued loveliness of arrangement was more agreeable to sense than Lehna Singh's ornate magnificence. A lace-like screen hung before a lofty recess. So plain it seemed that one wondered at seeing it motionless in the breeze made by the silken punkah swinging slowly to and fro before it. It was of most delicately wrought ivory, and veiled from the court where female attendants flitted noiselessly about a group of three persons engaged in earnest conversation. One, a woman whose black eyes had none of the languor of her race, reclined among embroidered cushions. The splendour of her jewels proclaimed the Ranee. Emeralds, rubies, and diamonds glittered on brow and arms. Before her on a cushion lay a carefully folded and voluminous letter. Lal Singh lolled at her side, and his gaze like hers was fixed on the ingenuous countenance of Atmâ Singh, who stood before the Ranee. She wore no veil, and as Atmâ encountered the gaze of her bold black eyes, he remembered the sneer of Lehna Singh.

"Come near," she commanded; "you come to me from our good friend, Lehna Singh. Let me hear what word you bring from him."

"I come, Maharanee," replied Atmâ modestly, "to obey your behests in all things, but especially to undertake a perilous mission, which I am assured will result in benefit to the faithful adherents of the Khalsa, as well as to the interests of your highness and the Maharajah."

"I have heard," said the Ranee, "much of your devotion, courage, and unswerving integrity, which render you peculiarly fitted for an enterprise requiring singular daring and fidelity. Lehna Singh has not scrupled to say that peril of life itself will even be welcome to so brilliant a spirit."

Her mocking tone brought the blood to Atmâ's cheek, he scarce knew why.

"It is the high calling of a Sikh," said he, "to encounter danger, and by the sword to confirm the Khalsa."

"It is a training that makes good soldiers," returned the Ranee, "but as my claims may prove less potent than those of the Khalsa, I promise that on your successful return you shall receive from my hands rare and costly jewels, and gold whose yellow lustre will bid the treasuries of the world to open."

"On the other hand," interrupted Rajah Lal, "remember that if we are betrayed, from that moment you are surrounded by countless and powerful foes, whose revenge you shall not elude."

The lion-heart of Atmâ beat high at this threat, to which he deigned no reply.

"My reward has been named, Maharanee," he said, "than which the world can hold no dearer. I will fulfil your embassy and return to you, but the prize for which I labour needs no enhancement to make it worthy."

The Maharanee sought the eye of her companion with a glance of satisfaction, but the Rajah's gaze was rivetted on Atmâ, whilst his features were distorted as if by a moment's uncontrollable rage. The transport passed as quickly as it had come, and he sank back to his former negligent posture. But the Ranee had seen, and a look of startled and angry intelligence lighted her eyes.

Her instructions bound Atmâ to convey to Golab Singh the letter before her, which Rajah Lal placed as she spoke in a casket. It was an expedition of some peril, as the country was occupied by the British and their native allies, to whom a messenger on his way to any court must be an object of suspicion. In addition to this the friendly reception at the Court of Jummoo of an envoy of Junda Kowr was altogether a matter of conjecture.

Further directions regarding his movements in Kashmir would, the Ranee informed him, be conveyed to him from time to time by trusted servants.

"A female servant," she said, "by name Nama, has frequently been employed by me on missions requiring great tact and caution. Her I will shortly send to the borders of Kashmir, and if you repair in fitting season to the Sacred Well of Purity you will there receive from her any communication I may have to make." The subject of the fateful sapphire she lightly dismissed. "If we receive through this slave a good report of the demeanour of this new-made Rajah, this horse-boy in my husband's service, Rajah Lal Singh will join you at the court of Kashmir, and the recovery of the missing jewel, which I am told forms a prominent ornament in Golab Singh's attire, will then no doubt engage the attention of you both."

At present it was evident that the introduction of an emissary of Junda Kowr into the councils of Golab Singh was the chief end in view. No thought of danger entered the heart of Atmâ as he went out from the presence of the Maharanee to enter upon an enterprise which was to be in its course and issue as unlike the anticipations of his ardent heart as is the solemn pilgrimage of life unknown to the dreams of childhood.

The affront of a threat and the alluring promises of riches were alike forgotten, and the star that led his exultant steps shone with the twofold radiance of love and loyalty.

Caroline Augusta Frazer

CHAPTER VII.

Atmâ directed his steps on the morning following his interview with Junda Kowr northward towards the confines of Kashmir. It was a lovely morning. A humid mist veiled the distant mountains, towards which his steps tended. Seen through its tender swaying folds, how vague and beautiful their savage slopes appeared. Light and shade, ominous gloom and shining crag were hid from view. How often thus the morn of life,

"In dim eclipse disastrous twilight sheds."

A twilight not dispelled until the light dawns on a retrospect whose bitterness could not be borne unless seen side by side with the other picture of Paradise.

But he had no thoughts other than of glad anticipation. Past pain and recent unrest were forgotten in the renewed joy of freedom. He cast care to the breeze for he had not lived long enough to know that the discontent which is the birthright of the children of Adam is not dependent on circumstances, but often attains most baleful activity when events seem least likely to harass the spirit. It was the morning of life and of love, and the obscurity in which youth walks is no dull haze but a golden glamour.

In one old form of the creation story is told the first utterance of Nature, the cry of chaos, "Let love be!" Through what inspiration of wisdom it comes to us out of the silence we do not know, but feel that the earlier tale of a divine mandate, "Light be!" is not at variance with it. The cry of chaos lingers in the heart of the race, and each new man in the morning of his being utters it in no doubt of its fulfilment in his own destiny. He loves mankind, and would be beloved; he loves nature, and perceives no relentless purpose in her variable moods; and perhaps most of all he loves his own soul with a love whose disenchantment is to be the sorest agony that an eternity can afford.

The cry of chaos lingers, and the story of creation is repeated in each life history. The cry meets with no response, but instead, relentlessly, surely, aye, and most mercifully, the facts and events group themselves about the cowering spirit, that before Love celestial Light may arise. It is a terrible destiny, devised by a God, and only possible in its severity for creatures to whom it has been declared, "Behold, ye are gods!"

At noon Atmâ rested beside a pool. It was a sequestered spot surrounded by thickets. The rushes grew rank and tall on the margin and in the water. The soft cooing of the doves hidden in the wood broke the stillness. He ate of the slender fare which he carried, and reclined on a flower couch until sleep closed his eyes. The doves cooed on, and bright lizards watched him.

Presently he awoke with a start. A rush of wind, a sudden plash of water were followed by the whizzing of an arrow through the air. He was close to the water. Softly peering through the reeds he saw, palpitating and stricken with fear, a snowy swan. The arrow had missed the stainless breast and it was unhurt. The wild creatures of his mountain home were dear to Atmâ, and he would fain shield the beautiful bird.

Two youths emerged from the thicket at some distance from where he stood. He went to meet them, smiling at the folly of his half-formed intention of guiding them from their prey. After courteous salutation they inquired whether he had seen the swan.

"It is a bird reared by ourselves," they said, "which strayed from us two days ago. We thought to wound it in the wing and recover it, but the creature is so wild that doubtless it is as well that it be killed out-right."

Atmâ had slept, he told them, had been aroused by their approach, had hardly realized the cause of his awakening. "The swan is difficult to rear," he said, "if indeed such effort be not fruitless."

"It is fruitless," they assented, "but we need not search hereabout if you have not seen it. You must have heard the flap of his wing had it alighted near you," and they turned their steps in a contrary direction. Atmâ watched their vain search until on the opposite side of the pool they disappeared into the wood.

He stole a glance into the hiding place of the swan. The soft plumage had not the dazzling purity which he had known, and the beautiful neck that should be proudly curved, drooped.

"Poor imprisoned creature," he thought, "grown in bondage, alien to its own nature of strength and beauty."

He watched it unperceived, timidly washing its plumage in the still deep water. Soon it floated further from the bank. Now and then it waited and listened. The story of its captivity was told again in its stealthy, trembling happiness.

But high overhead, between it and a disc of blue sky, intervened a stream of lordly birds flying south. From their ranks wafted a cry, and as it fell there rose a wild echo, an unfamiliar note from the captive swan. It rose skyward, wearied wing and broken spirit forgotten. It might be danger, but it was Home, and like a disembodied spirit it ascended to a life that, altogether new, was to be for the first time altogether familiar.

A thought of kindred saddened the heart of Atmâ. In the loss of parents and brethren lay, he thought, the sole cause of the heaviness that oppressed him. Their restoration would have made existence complete. He had lost them before he had awakened to the knowledge that those we love are even, when nearest, very far away. Humanity does not hear the voice of kindred on earth.

I find

In all the earth
Like things with like combined,
How happy, happy from their birth
Are silly things, in guileless mirth
Who seek them out and greatly love their kind.
How e'en
The crafty snake,
Like dove of gentle mien,
Doth with his fellows converse take
The love-notes well from wood and brake
That tell betwixt some lives some barriers intervene.
Ah me,
Shall only one
Of golden things that be,
One only underneath the sun
In dolour here life's journey run,
Speeding the way alone to great Eternity?
The Soul
It sits apart,
Craving a prison dole
Of ruth and healing for its hurt,
As piteous captive should cajole,
Vainly, unheeding ear afar in stranger mart.

CHAPTER VIII.

One night Atmâ dreamed a dream which greatly disturbed his waking thoughts. He lay in the shadow of an overhanging rock, and in deep sleep fancied that he descried therein a door which was securely barred. But although it was closed, there issued from it aroma of most subtle perfumes, which seemed to enter the brain and incite the energies to a maddening desire of possession, while there floated around him strains of music whose sweetness filled the soul with sorrow of itself. In his dream he tried the heavy bolts in vain. All was fast. He yielded to despair, and dashed himself against the rocky portal in anguish of disappointment. But grief wore itself out, and he thought that he presently lay on the ground, bruised and exhausted. The charmed fragrance still enwrapt him, and the seductive melody filled the air. Sad and benumbed he yielded himself to their influence, and his ear then detected in the ethereal harmony an articulate utterance. An ineffable intonation melodiously spoke:

"It opes to a key that is golden,
Within it a spirit lies folden,
The soul of all matchless delight.
All graces familiar or olden,
Propitious thine entrance invite."

He now dimly perceived the golden key to glitter in the air. It came near to him, and he took it into his hand from where it lay on a pillow of mist. When he held it, the rocky door, though still fastened, no longer hid from view the loveliness of the grotto. He saw walls bedecked with gleaming jewels, marvellous flowers, and countless silver lamps, whilst everywhere were traced in precious gems the sayings of the Wise of all ages. Winged creatures, whose looks spoke of loving and perfect service, seemed to await his command.

A great fear seized him lest so beautiful a vision should presently fade, and he would have rushed to unbar the entrance, his eyes dimming with tears of love and sorrow. But a second voice sounded from above more solemnly sweet than the first—

"Beware! beware!
To abide none enter there;
All you see is but a portal
Leading on to the Immortal;
Though it be so fair, so fair,
Enter, not to tarry there;
Idle tears, your torrent stay—
Beauty, it is consecrate
And can never fade away;
Change it will, be re-create,
Born from narrow things to great."

But the first voice pleaded again. Together they sang, and strangely enough they harmonized. Not that the celestial utterance lent itself to the lighter measure, but the nearer song took a softer cadence and borrowed a new persuasion from the greater. Passionate grew the pleading, more alluring the radiant retreat. The heart of Atmâ, ever open to the influence of the good, cried to the solemn voice above for help.

"Give also light," he said, "that I may see beyond the portal!"

But the sound of his own voice was strange in the land of dreams, and with that he awoke. It was evening, and he arose and looked at the silent and frowning cliff, and even passed his hand over its face to convince himself that he was still awake. A significance attached itself to his dream, and he pondered it long and wisely. The teachings of the founder of his Faith came into his mind, and the lesson of his vision seemed plain. He resolved to trust the conduct of his steps to an unseen Guidance, and reverently owned that a Benign Presence had watched his slumbers. As he reflected, a belief grew that this massive rock marked not only a halting place in his journey, but a chief interval in his life.

"The way," he said, "is very long. Of what use but to mislead in that course is my bodily sight, which bids me doubt the reality of all the higher truths which my inner consciousness affirms?"

The stars were coming out, and looking upward he remembered his childhood's hope that beyond their radiant ranks was the Home of Spirits, and thus he prayed:

"Father of Lights, these lesser beacons hide,
My way is long, this desert plain is wide,
Darken mine eyes so I behold my guide.
The way is long, it leads among the stars.
How should I roam that shimmering vault of night?
How halt where yon bright orb his lamp uprears
In glistering chains of light,
To list 'mid ringing spheres for that strange psalm?
The sum of agony were surely this—
To hear the Blessed Wind 'mid waving palm;
The pearly gates to miss
Whose glorious light is not of moon nor sun;
To list the river's flow, and stand undone.
Light of the Realms of bliss, be Thou mine eye;
So shall my homeless soul, when death is nigh,
With joy a mansion in the heavens descry."

Caroline Augusta Frazer

CHAPTER IX.

As Atmâ drew near to the confines of Kashmir he trod a secluded vale, and followed the windings of a broad stream whose banks were thickly wooded. As he pursued his way through a thicket he heard voices in gay converse, and stayed his steps until, peering through the heavy foliage, he descried below the overhanging river-bank two dark-eyed girls. They were seated on a broad stone, and one laved her feet in the water and bent over the swift current; but the head of the other, wreathed in scarlet blossoms, was uplifted, and in the bright face half turned towards him he recognized an attendant of Moti. She listened as if suspecting his approach, but soon apparently satisfied, she resumed her light chatter with her companion. Atmâ heard his own name, and gathered that they sought him. He made himself known, and the elder, who was Nama, the Maharanee's trusted servant, related how her mistress greatly desiring a sprig of White Ak, a tree of great virtue in incantations, had commissioned her to obtain it in the forest near by. She had also been charged, she said, to meet Atmâ Singh, and bring her illustrious mistress tidings of his welfare.

Although, as a true Sikh, Atmâ worshipped an Idea, and held in scorn all material semblance of the supernatural, he knew that magic was largely practised by professed adherents of the Khalsa, and so heard her errand without surprise, though guessing that its timely performance had in view some other purpose concerning himself. This became certain when Nana made known to him that she was not then to return home, but to linger here and in the neighbourhood of the Sacred Well, spoken of by the Ranee, for an indefinite time, while the girl beside her at once returning, would bear to Ferazpore as well as to the house of his uncle tidings of his present safety. As Nama spoke, Atmâ fancied once that the little maid standing by sought to engage his attention by a mute sign, but, ere he could be sure, she desisted and became engrossed in the adjustment of the crown of scarlet flowers with which she had bedecked her head. A dim suspicion of treachery rose in his breast, a vague misgiving. He rapidly recalled to mind the affectionate language of his kinsman, the promises of the Ranee, and perhaps stronger than all rose the dear vanity of royal youth, which cannot believe itself scorned. Were not all the high hopes of his life at stake? It is not possible that when youth hazards all, the venture should fail. But the foreboding remained. It was akin to the shudder which tells us that some one steps on the sod beneath which we are to lie. The analysis of these subtle melancholies is hard to read. A breath may summon them and they linger unbidden, and whether they point only to the dim shadows they invoke from the past, or whether their warning be of the future, we cannot say. Even as I write a sadness oppresses me, born of I know not what.

> If any asked me whence it came,
> This languor of my soul to-day,
> And why I muse in piteous frame
> While all the glowing world is gay,
> I could not tell, I only mourn,
> And wonder how to life it stirred,
> The memory of that distant morn,
> As then I wondered had I heard
> That grief could ever sink to sleep
> Nor aye that stony vigil keep.
> Enter ye dreams of vanished woe,
> The spectral griefs of long ago;
> I fold my hands, in dreamlike trance,
> I see their shadowy train advance—
> Phantom forms like shades of eld,

Memory-prints or forms beheld,
I cannot know, they fade away;
Faintly their voices seem to say,
"You loved us not that distant day,"
And, lo, my foolish tears o'erflow.
Can this be I who fain would know
Those bitter griefs of long ago?

As Atmâ approached the city of Jummoo he found himself again by a river-side, and seeing a small boat he entered it and was soon gliding with the current. It was night when he floated among the trees of the Palace gardens. Thousands of lights glittered through the foliage. The air was burdened with perfume. High above the sombre umbrage rose slender snowy spires, around which the moonbeams lingered lovingly. He left the little skiff and trod the terraced ascent. A meandering brooklet, tributary of the larger stream, was spanned by fairy-like bridges. He hesitated among the intersecting ways, mazy, enchanting, and flower-bordered. The living air was full of subdued sound. Bubbling water, tinkling bells, and the mingling of many voices made music which was borne on perfumed winds. This was the fairest spot in all sunny Kashmir, where the nightingale sings perpetually in groves of citron, magnolia, and pomegranate.

He reached the splendid portico which was the chief entrance of the Palace. Its carven and gilded roof was supported by alabaster columns. It had been a day of pomp and festival, and courtiers still in their yellow robes of state reclined here, languidly enjoying the cool night air. Atmâ ascended the broad steps where officers of state were marshalled in lines, gold-hilted swords at their sides, and their gorgeous attire glittering with jewels. Here he requested an audience of the Rajah, and, preceded by a servant bearing his credentials, he passed through lofty and magnificent chambers to an ante-room where he rested until summoned to the presence of Golab Singh, whom he found in an inner court lit by rose-hued lamps. The air was cool, delicious and fragrant, the stillness and the softened light were in pleasing contrast to the dazzling splendour of the halls and room he had traversed. Here in an alcove were seated three or four men. The Maharajah received him with affability, and made gravely courteous enquiries for the health and well-being of Junda Kowr. He welcomed her envoy, and would know of the difficulties and dangers of his journey thither, and added graceful flattery to his commiseration. Then, after much courteous discourse, he confided the young Sikh to the care of attendants, with many injunctions regarding his comfort and refreshment. And Atmâ went out from the august presence with heart elate, for he had instantly observed in the turban of Golab Singh a gem which by its size and hue he knew must be none other than the Sapphire of Fate, whose magical renown might yet in his true hands rally a degenerate Khalsa until such time as the disciples of Nanak might again know good from evil, and reverence Truth alone.

An hour later, as he left the sumptuous baths where obsequious slaves had attended him, an officer of state approached him with a message from the Rajah.

"Atmâ Singh, there are within these walls Englishmen who hold command in the British army. As a true friend and servitor to the Ranee, and the Maharajah's esteemed guest, do not divulge nor let them suspect that you had lately audience of her highness."

For Golab Singh, notwithstanding the cruelty of his administration, was friend to all, Christian, Musselman, Brahmin, or Sikh, and did not love to be suspected of an undue sympathy with any, not even when such sympathy might wear the cloak of patriotic loyalty.

CHAPTER X.

On the morrow the Rajah of Kashmir sat in the terraced garden and talked of life. Those who sat with him had lately braved death on battlefield, but death had forborne to touch them, and they rejoiced in existence. All around them the story was repeated; the deepening shade spoke of another shadow, but the flashing sunbeams chased the thought ere it chilled; eaves fluttering to the mould said, "Ponder the grave," but the shining air stirred and sent them whirling aloft. Death and Life enacted a drama.

The human comedy ends in woe, but Nature tenderly masks her catastrophe, and her sorrows are hung with gayest colours and adorned with fairest effects. This is seen at sunset. The evening saddens, the earth melts, and in my egoism I hail a fellow mourner. I would protract the moment of the sun's entombment.

"There's such a charm in melancholy,

I would not if I could be gay."

It is the mood of little griefs. An unquiet wind murmurs, but it does not rise to a wail.

I fain would bid th' Æolian tones prolong

To mourn the jolly Day's discomfiture,

And, mindful of mine own estate, among

The buds and grieving trees my plaint outpour,

That sweets must fade though Night will aye endure.

But crafty Nature, fancy to beguile

From her disaster, which, alas! is mine,

Bids to the front in radiant defile

A trooping host whose pomps incarnadine

The faded trophies of the dying day,

And, lest I fail before so brave array,

She decks the quiet clouds where fancies dwell

With sweet translucent gleam and melting hue
To woo my swooning sense with softer spell
Of blissful pink and hyacinthine blue.

"Life," said the Rajah, "is the fairest of flowers, and its beauty and fragrance are for him who plucks."

"Plucks," sighed one, "to find it wither in his grasp."

Said the Rajah, "To do justice to life, one must forget death."

"Forgetfulness may be desirable," said another, "but how shall it be attained? How deny the tyrant who at each sunset demands his tribute dues of sleep, and enwraps my vassal being in dull oblivion?"

"By ill-conditioned fears," replied the Rajah, "men invite evil. To him who desires the solace of ghostly companionship shall the spectres troop, a phantom in every shadow, and with him make their abode. He who fears is already overcome. To the man who would live there must be no death. For me, I love the rosy, teeming present; to-morrow is with the gods, and I for one," he added laughing, "will not be guilty of an impious theft by anticipating their gifts."

"Life," said an Englishman, "is a battle-field in which victory is to the valiant. To my mind the effort after forgetfulness is no less disquieting than the fear you would shun. Death, could we but believe it, is simple and natural as Life."

But this he said, not knowing that

"Life is a mystery as deep as ever death can be."

"It is true," spoke the Venerable Nawab Khan, a Musselman of devout piety, "and to what purpose do we struggle? The inevitable is not to be averted

Tho', sliding through lush grass, the shining snake,
Loving the sun, a sinuous way doth take,
Its fixed journey to its home 'twill make.
Even as in tranquil vale reluctant rill,
In sportive twinings nigh its parent hill,

Proceedeth onward to the ocean still.

"Life is a dream," continued the pious man, "and the first condition of its happiness is peace. For me I am weary of battle-fields, and feel no desire to grasp after illusive flowers and fading grass. If anticipated evil is the shadow of life, the vain toils of restless ambition are its menace. Vain toil it is! To labour, to suffer, to sorely strive that we may accomplish—our destiny! For that is what our utmost effort alike with our quietude will achieve."

"And," demanded the Rajah, "is it then life to breathe? Such tranquillity will breed torpor rather than dream. If the immobility of Fate be the theme and burden of my days I dare the more. Let us bare our breasts to the arrows of Fortune, let us invite the shafts of Chance, let us taunt Fate, let us dare our doom, why should we fear? The hands of Destiny are also bound, and not one pang the more shall we feel for our hardihood."

But one who reclined on a couch of roses and breathed their languorous fragrance, chided the fervency of this discourse, saying:

"If Life be a flower,
Light, facile, and free,
Be the grasp that would hold it;
From a halcyon sea
Let the breezes that stir it
Blow thoughtlessly;
No breath of care should chill it,
Nor sad foreboding thrill it,
For honey-dew lies hid
Beneath a fragile lid,
And ardent clutch will spill it."

"Ay," cried the Rajah, "I like the counsel of the flowers.
Obeissance to the blast
Make, mock when it is past,

And rise like a washen rose, deliciously,
Forgetful of sorrow,
Unheeding the morrow,
And meeting all destinies, mad, merrily;
If Life be a flower, 'tis fairest of all
If for it you fear fortune's pitiless thrall,
With the Tulip's proud beauty
Its wisdom combine,
And bear to the contest
A goblet of wine!"

"Ah," sighed the pensive one, "but the flower is the poppy, for he who possesses it presently falls asleep."

But his gentle conceit was unheard, for Nawab Khan related a story.

"One sought," said he, "the cave where dwelt a holy hermit of great reputation for wisdom and learning. He sate him down before the entrance, and listened with patience and fortitude to the grave and weighty saws which like bats increase in darkness. Having presently earned the right of a disciple, he plied the sage with questions, as:—What is the material and constitution of the soul? Where are laid the bones of Seth? What bounds the credulity of mankind? These and many more did the Wise answer in difficult words whose sound carried conviction. 'He knows all things,' thought the inquirer, 'I need not to ply him with riddles to whom all things are plain. I will rather seek counsel for myself concerning what lies at hand.' With that he put the question, 'What think you of human life?' The hermit, who had halted hitherto at no question, arose, turned him about, and in silence withdrew to the depths of his grotto."

"Proving," laughed the Rajah, "that he added the virtue of discretion to his multiform merits. But we turn not our backs on the question until my illustrious guest Atmâ Singh of the blood of the Holy Nanak further expound the nature of life."

All turned to Atmâ. The frivolity of the Rajah was distasteful to him in connection with so grave a theme. His eyes involuntarily sought the glance of the young Englishman who had spoken. He was an officer in the British army and his name was Bertram. His expressive face kindled with kindly grace as the young Sikh claimed sympathy with him in his view of life as a battlefield.

"But not," said Atmâ, "that triumph crowns prowess in this fight. I know that life is a battle in which sooner or later we must all succumb, but we die knowing that the right is stronger through our struggle."

"I am rebuked, Atmâ Singh," said Bertram; "your battlefield is a nobler one than that on which human effort is rewarded by gain. I pray you continue."

"Behold the strength that comes from a convert," sneered some of the company, as with fervent though modest speech Atmâ spoke of the high courage and dauntless faith which transform defeat into Immortal victory.

A silence fell on the gay throng. Some were gloomy because reminded of their national discomfiture. Others looked coldly on Atmâ and muttered with discontent—

"He speaks of life as a thing that is yet to be."

CHAPTER XI.

Rajah Lal Singh arrived at Jummoo a few weeks later in much pomp and state. No hidden or hazardous mission was his. His gorgeous train of armed attendants mounted on richly caparisoned horses traversed the public roads, winding like a brilliant serpent through the vales of Kashmir. He brought tidings of the daily increasing quiet and peace now resting on the torn and war-spent Punjaub. Festivities were heightened after his arrival, and revelry held sway day and night.

Atmâ and Bertram in unconscious kinship drew to one another, forsaking frequently the mirth and glare of the court to converse of things that are hard to understand. They were one evening in a shady retreat at the foot of the Rajah's terraced gardens.

"I confess," said Atmâ, "that the fixedness of fate engages my thought frequently, though hitherto unprofitably. No doubt the teachers of your land have spoken and written much on a subject so perplexing."

"They have," replied Bertram; "it has ever been a favourite whetstone for the human reason. It has been frequently solved to the satisfaction of the performer, but no solution has yet won the universal acceptance that is the badge of truth."

"It may be," said Atmâ, "that the answer lies not anywhere beneath our sky."

A rustle in the foliage behind them drew the attention of both. A gleam of vivid colour was visible when they quickly turned, and Atmâ was in the act of parting the myrtle boughs, when, anticipating him, Lal Singh stepped forth from retreat. Silken attire and splendour of jewelled turban were insufficient to dignify his crestfallen demeanour, which, however, changed rapidly when he darted a glance of rage and hate at Bertram, who had greeted his sudden appearance with a scornful laugh.

"No doubt," he said, "the English Sahib and Atmâ Singh have grave secrets whose discussion calls for deep retirement."

"No doubt of it," laughed Bertram, "but, Rajah Lal, the yellow vestments of a noble Sikh," for the Rajah wore his state dress, "are so ill fitted for ambuscade that I promptly refuse to admit you to our councils."

What answer the Rajah, whose stealthy face grew livid at this sally, might have made, was stopped by Atmâ, who, well aware of the danger to his companion from such an enemy, and all unknowing of his own place in the Rajah's esteem, interposed with courteous speech.

"We are on our way," said he, "to the Muslim burial-place near by, the tombs of which have become interesting through the tales of Nawab Khan. Bertram Sahib jests, we will be gratified by Rajah Lal Singh joining us."

The Rajah had regained self-possession and declined the proffered courtesy in his usual cold and sneering manner, adding with a crafty smile and with covert meaning, which perplexed and startled Bertram:

"It is a wise man who familiarizes himself with the grave. For me, I must deny myself, for I go tomorrow to take part in festivities the reverse of funereal. I commend the propriety and aptness of your researches, Atmâ Singh."

So saying he withdrew with a salaam that failed to cover the swift scowl he bestowed on Bertram.

"There goes an enemy, Atmâ Singh," said Bertram, watching the retreating figure arrayed in barbaric splendour, the profusion of the enormous emeralds that adorned his yellow robe so subduing its hue that Bertram's thrust was unmerited, as far as his attire was concerned at least. "He is a foe to fear, unless I greatly mistake, an enemy of the serpent kind," he continued.

But they speedily forgot the craft of the serpent, and pursued their walk, conversing as they went.

Some tenets, they found, were familiar to the minds of both, and these, they observed, might be called historical. Such were the vague whisperings of things that occurred in the dawn of young Time before the earliest twilight of story—traditions that linger as shades among the nations, vague hints of former greatness and of a calamity, a crime whose enormity is guessed by the magnitude of its shadow hovering over the earth, shrouding men's cradles and darkening with a menace their tombs. Such too were the joyful surmisings of a restoration, such the imaginings of

"That bright eternal day
Of which we priests and poets say
Such truths as we expect for happy men."

"Your story of the world's creation is strangely in accord with ours," said Bertram. "Our narrative is more precise, but the things stated so clearly typify we know not what; and we and you are, I doubt not, wisest when we own ourselves ignorant. Who can tell what is implied in the tale of the birth of Time out of Eternity, ascending through seven gradations to we know not what consummation when this seventh epoch of rest shall be run?"

"The words of the wise," said Atmâ, "assign to all things perpetuity, which involves a repetition of the cycle of Seven. Does the week of seven days repeating itself endlessly in time, image the seven epochs which, returning again and again, may constitute eternity?"

Bertram paused before he replied—

"Your words move me, Atmâ Singh, for I have heard that on the first day of a new week a Representative Man rose from the dead."

They reached the Burying Ground. It was a lovely spot. Fallen into disuse, the bewitching grace of carelessness was added to the architectural beauty of the tombs. The verdure was rank, and luxuriant trees and marble tombs alike were festooned with clematis and jasmine. Here they were pleased to find Nawab Khan and the servant, whom he dismissed on their arrival, and himself guided them to an old tomb simpler in form than the rest, but more tenderly and beautifully clothed in moss and wild flowers than any. They sat down while the Nawab related the story of the maiden whose goodness it commemorated.

"Sangita," said he, "was a princess of incomparable beauty and surpassing gentleness. Her spirit was humble; and as the heavenly streams of wisdom and virtue seek lowly places, her nature shone every day with a purer lustre. She loved tenderly a gazelle which she had reared, and which was the companion of her happy hours. It was not of the King's flocks but had been found in Sangita's own garden, and none knew who had brought it there. The talkative people, noting the sagacity of the pretty creature and the tender solicitude of its mistress, who crowned it anew with garlands every morning and fed it with sweetest milk and the loveliest flower buds, whispered to one another of its mysterious appearance, and alleged for it miraculous origin. One day as it fed among lilies, the princess near by, overcome by the heat, slumbered. She slept long and heavily, and when she awoke her favourite was nowhere to be seen. Calling and weeping, she wandered through vale and glade, searching the hare's covert, but starting back, for she descried a viper there; peering into the den of a wild beast and shuddering, for it was strewn with bones; hastening to a gorgeous clump of bloom where she thought it might have rested, but the splendid blossoms were poisonous and she turned away. All the dark, damp, dangerous night she sought, and it was morning when she found the gentle creature stretched on the moss, its piteous eyes glazed over with death, for it had been pursued and had sunk from exhaustion.

In delirious ravings Sangita told her people that when she knelt on the moss, and, wringing her hands, bewailed that it had not sought the shelter of a Secure Resting Place, the gazelle reproached her.

'I know not of that country,' it said, 'it is not here.'

And this, although the wild speech of a fevered brain, gained credit with the populace, and the Wild Gazelle cherished by the good princess became a memory fraught with awe and superstition. For me, I believe that the devout and good heart utters wisdom unawares, and that the tongue habituated to golden speech may drop riches even when the light of reason is withdrawn. The sickness of Sangita was mortal, but her mind cleared before she expired, and she then obtained from the King her father a promise that over her ashes should be erected a lodge whose door, never fastened, might afford a Haven of Retreat such as her fevered dream desired!"

They looked on the tomb, its walls gleamed white through the foliage that draped it. It was old and neglected. The door was nearly concealed from view by the luxuriant growth of many years, and when they examined it closely they found that it hung on one rusty hinge.

"May we believe," asked Bertram, "that the tender fancy of the dying princess was ever verified by the actual shelter here of a fugitive?"

"The story is ancient," replied Nawab Khan, "and I cannot say. The lesson she taught would forbid the finding anywhere a Place of Rest."

But it neared the hour of the devout man's prayers and he left them.

"Nawab Khan," said Atmâ, "speaks not as he believes, for many are the Havens of the Mohammedan."

"Ay," said Bertram, "and does not every creed too soon become a secure retreat to the spirit of man to which God has denied the repose of certainty. We crave knowledge which is withheld more earnestly than we desire faith or hope, and we eagerly make even its semblance a foothold. It appears to me, my friend, with whom I am grown bold, that you and I may find in our less material beliefs as false a haven as the pilgrim finds in his Mecca."

"You say well," said Atmâ thoughtfully, "it is not new to me. Thoughts for which I cannot account have been borne in upon my soul, waking and sleeping, by riverside or on mountain height, and I know and believe that he who would find God must close his eyes and his ears."

"And the soul," said Bertram, "that knows an infallible guide, be it voice of other man, or of his own reason, or volume of mystery, or whatever it be, that soul walks not by faith. But why speak of a soul finding God? The soul of man must be first found of Him, and it seems to me that until thus adopted no soul would prefer faith to knowledge—thus much might we learn of Nawab Khan."

And as they returned to the Palace, they continued this grave discourse, lamenting the sadness and sin of the world, and Atmâ, greatly moved, told that his life's purpose, of which he might not fully speak, involved the conquest of evil and the redemption of the world by means whose greatness was worthy of the end. And Bertram, sometimes assenting, often silent, hoped that at last, by each and all means employed by man, the whole world might be redeemed. He was a Christian and devout, but he, too, desired to redeem the world. His dream was one with Atmâ's. But the highest dreams are soonest dissolved, for the dispelling of illusions and breaking of idols is God's benison, and is given soonest to those whom He approves.

CHAPTER XII.

There was fear of Evil Influence, pestilence and death in the country, and as the time of new moon drew near, propitiatory sacrifices were prepared. A number of the courtiers of Golab Singh declared their intention of visiting sacred places and offering gifts. Many who abjured these rites went also as to a festival. On such an errand many supposed Lal Singh to be gone, although his prolonged absence led to unspoken surmisings among those who looked on him as the emissary of a political party, but at the close of a fierce contest men are chary of speech, and none spoke his suspicions. At all events he had disappeared the day after the events of our last chapter.

Atmâ resolved to take this opportunity of attempting to communicate with the Maharanee, and intimated his purpose of resorting to the Well designated by Nama. It was of course on the southern border of Kashmir, and entailed a long pilgrimage. Bertram, tired of splendour, would accompany him. Together they set out on horseback, followed by attendants who bore gifts for the Shrine. They rode forward, leaving their retinue, and conversed as was their wont.

Atmâ fain would know why his friend so devoutly went on pilgrimage.

"I suppose," said Bertram laughing, "that the Nawab would tell you, though the ass goes to Mecca he becomes not a pilgrim thereby. But Atmâ Singh, if I mistake not, your own creed does not recognize the rites we are to witness; I ask, then, in my turn, why, since our mission is meaningless, does your choice of a destination lead us to the most distant of the sacred places?"

"I do not say that the Shrine is without sanctity to me," replied Atmâ evasively, "and the place is one of great attractiveness, while the journey thither, though longer, is more agreeable than other routes. But your jesting challenge reminds me of what once befel the holy Nanak, the founder of the Sikh religion. He slept in the heat of the day on a grassy bank with his feet turned westward. A Mohammedan priest finding him, struck him and demanded how he dared direct his feet towards the sacred city of Mecca. 'How dare you, infidel dog, to turn your feet towards God?' he demanded. The wise one responded:

'Though past the highest heaven of heavens I rise,
Though cowering in the deep I hide mine eyes,
I roam but through the Mosque his hands have wrought,
Show me, O Moulvie, where thy God is not!'"

"Your wise man spoke a great truth," said Bertram. "The earth is a Temple, it was designed for a House of Prayer, and in it God has placed not a sect nor a nation, but all mankind. Many a Holy of Holies has man raised within this temple, and vainly have the builders sought by every device of loveliness, sensuous or shadowy, to achieve for their inventions the Beauty of Holiness. Your Nanak was divinely taught, for leaving alike the Material and the Ideal, he grasped the True."

Now they paused where sat a mendicant who besought charity. Atmâ bestowed a gift, saying,

"Our great teacher said:

'The beggar's face a mirror is, in it
We best learn how our zeal in heaven appears.
Pause then and look—nor pious alms omit,
Lest on its brightness fall an angel's tears.'"

Then Bertram, pleased with this, asked more regarding the founder of the Sikh faith, and Atmâ related what things the teacher had accounted holy. "This," he said, "did he instruct:

'The hearts that justice and soft pity shrine
Are the true Mecca, loved of the Divine.
Who doth in good deeds duteous hours engage,
Performs for God an holy pilgrimage.
Who to his own hurt speaks the truth, he tells
The Mystic Speech that pious rite excels.
Rude orisons of alien He will bless
If they are offered but in faithfulness.'"

"It is good," said Bertram, "modes of worship are many, faiths are nearly as various as the temperaments of mankind, but virtue is one. No universal intuition prompts to a form of ritual as acceptable to God, but the moral sense of all the race points unswervingly to the pole-star of the soul—Truth, another name for Purity.

"Many," he continued, "have been the self-ordained guides of the human conscience, blind leaders of the blind, would-be saviours of the world! Why should a mazed wandering soul be so eager to summon followers, so ready to point the way? What strange prompting of love or daring is here? It surely is not from desire of applause that men seek the leadership on the road to heaven, for what man so decried in the history of the world as he who arrogates to himself the place and name of Priest? And yet priest and poet are akin. The man who seeks the place of mediator and interpreter betwixt his fellows and the Unknowable must needs be an idealist, and if he deal with illusion who so unfortunate as he?"

They halted that night where two streams met. Bathed in moonlight it was a scene of great beauty and repose, a confluence of the beatitudes of earth and air. Peace filled their souls so that they perceived the unexpressive adoration of the river, and the trees, and the solemn moonlight. It was such an hour as makes poets of men, and Atmâ raised his head and spoke:

"At tranquil eve is proper time for prayer,
When winds are fair,
And gracious shadows 'mong the myrtles move.
The list'ning eve it was ordained for prayer.
By the soft murmur of thy cooing dove
Teach me to love;
Grant that thy starry front fill my death's night
With joyful light;
And hushed as on this bank the violet's close
Be my repose.
Abide Love, Happiness, and Peace till shining morn
From the same birth that gave the past be borne."
Bertram:
"Fair are these hillside haunts at even calm,
And sweet the fragrance of each flowery spray.
Dew of the Spirit, fall in heavenly balm
Upon my slumbers; bounteous Lord, I pray,
Like one who sang thy praise in other way,
Bless Thou the wicked, for the Good, I know,
Are blessed already, blessed they come and go."

CHAPTER XIII.

The shrine of the Well of Purity was on a dainty islet which lay in the centre of a small lake. The grotto was almost concealed from view, but moving forms of worshippers were visible among the trees when Atmâ and Bertram drew near to the water's edge. A band of laughing girls carrying laden baskets of corn, and rice, and flowers were leaving the shore in a light skiff. It was a lovely scene, the shining lake reflecting again the gem-like mound of foliage which rested on its breast. Bertram gazed on the picture, whilst Atmâ, whose quick and expectant eyes had discerned the form of Nama near at hand, followed her unnoticed by his companion. The Maharanee, Nama related, had sent to Atmâ Singh the gold which she carried, in token of her approval of her loyal servitor, and also a box of onyx which she prayed him to open and read words contained therein, retaining meanwhile possession of the casket and its contents until further tidings. With many reverences Nama further informed him that the Fairest of all the Lilies pined for him, was grieving at his absence, but was now to be gladdened by the prospect of his speedy return, which tidings the Maharanee had deputed her to convey forthwith to the household of Lehna Singh. Notwithstanding the joy of knowing himself an object of tender solicitude, a vague foreboding once again filled the soul of Atmâ. When the woman left him he considered thoughtfully the messages he had just received, slowly meanwhile undoing the claspings of the onyx box and raised the lid. Immediately a powerful odour issued from it and almost overcame him. He reeled and gasped for breath, nearly losing consciousness. However, having seated himself, he presently recovered, and somewhat more cautiously opening the casket, he drew from it a paper which contained a strangely worded commendation of himself, "The staunch and courageous friend of the Ranee, the Restorer of the Sapphire of Fate, the foe of whatever was inimical or false to the Sikh interest." Thought Atmâ, "This praise is no doubt won by the good report conveyed to her by Lal Singh, who, notwithstanding faults, can be generous as well as just to a Sikh brother."

He remained seated for some time, his head supported on his hand, for he still felt giddy, thinking painfully and earnestly. The numbing effects of the odour he had inhaled testified to its poisonous nature, but no precautions, he reflected, had been taken to ensure its effect; on the contrary, its immediate result was to alarm and warn the rash meddler ere mischief could be wrought. Nama also had hastened away, as not expecting any such terrible issue, of which certain tidings would be desired if murder such as he dreamed of had been contemplated. It could not be, he thought, and Rajah Lal would explain on his return what now appeared so mysterious.

Returning the paper to its case he secured it about his attire and sought Bertram, who had wandered along the woody banks of the lake, and whom he found at some distance away, listening to the rare song of a swan, distant and strange and sweet. Soon it glided into death at the opposite shore. It brought back to Atmâ's mind the morning when a noble bird had by his aid escaped its captors. He recalled its subsequent restoration to its kind, and the sympathy and undefined aspirations awakened in his breast.

They entered a boat and crossed the water, landing speedily on the soft, damp islet sward. The grotto was still clad in morning freshness, for the strong beams of the sun had not yet penetrated to the heart of the sacred grove. The entrance was hung with garlands, votive offerings from the poorer pilgrims. More costly gifts lay near and all around knelt worshippers.

A new party arrived, bringing a snowy fleeced lamb to be offered in sacrifice. It was decked with wreaths, and bleated piteously.

Presently it was killed, and its blood was caught in vessels to be taken home and smeared on doors and walls to drive away blight and pestilence from the dwellings of men. While this was being done, the crowd looked on carelessly or curiously. But Bertram and Atmâ noticed that the man who had made this offering looked upwards with famished eyes and despairing, and a groan escaped his lips, and to Bertram it seemed as if he said:

"Behold I go forward, but he is not there; and backward, but I cannot perceive him."

They stood apart, watching the scene. Then Atmâ presented his gift for the enriching of the shrine, and withdrawing aside he knelt on the grass and prayed,

"Bright God and Only God!
Not to be understood!
Illume the darkened twilight of thine earth;
The dewdrop of so little worth
Is garnished from the riches of the sun;
Lead me from shadowy things to things that be,
Lest, all undone,
I lose in dreams my dream's reality;
Thy Home is in the Fatherland of Light,
Strong God and Bright!
In still beatitude and boundless might!
I veil mine eyes,
Thy holy Quietness I seek with sighs."

Said Bertram, "The earth has not a spectacle more fraught with meaning than this; the acknowledged monarch of terrestrial things bowing in dread—a dread of what? of that voice in his breast which, being silent, is yet the loudest thing he knows? Why is the innocence of that sacrificial lamb so pathetic to my sight? Why should religious rites in which I do not participate move me strangely and deeply?"

"These things are a shadow," said Atmâ, "and a shadow is created by a fact."

"I join in your prayer," said Bertram. "'Lead me from shadowy things to things that be.' Types are not for him who believes that the horizon of his sight bounds the possible."

"No," replied Atmâ, "better reject the image than accept it as the end of our desire. The faith of my fathers, which grasped after Truth, teaches me that if the outward semblance of divine verities lead captive not only my senses, to which its appeal is made, but my heart's allegiance, I am guilty of idolatry."

"How fair," said Bertram, "must be the thing imaged by earth's loveliest pageantry! What must be the song of whose melody broken snatches and stray notes reach us in the golden speech of those endowed with hearing to catch its echoes! What harmony of beatitude is taught by the mystery of heavenly colour! How dull must be our faculties, or how distant the bliss for which our souls yearn as from behind a lattice, seeing only as in a mirror of burnished silver, which, though it be never so bright, reflects but dimly! How unutterable are our transitory glimpses of eternal possibilities!"

"Therein," said Atmâ, "may lie the reason why evanescent beauty stirs us most. It may be more heavenly in meaning or affinity than things that remain. This has sometimes perplexed me.

"For, ever most our love is given
To glories whose decadence fleet
Has more of changeful earth than heaven;
The heart's astir,
And sympathies leap forth to greet
The mingling fair
Of heavenly hues limned in empyreal bow
Aloft in dewy air, but ere we know

Their place and method true they fade away,
And fancy follows still, though things as beauteous stay.
What joyous note,
Warbled in bliss of upper air,
May with the one death-song compare
That floats among the reeds, and blends
With wild wind's plaint, till silence ends
In haunt remote
Sweet life and song;
They float away the reeds among.

"I beware me of types," he continued, "though I know nothing real. I am surrounded by images, my present state of being is a shadow, but I crave reality. The symbol is fair, but Truth is fairer. To that verity all types must yield, how beautiful soever they be, or meet to express their burden."

And yet how dear the transient joys of time,
Their purport not the Pearl of our desire.
Loved are these confines as immortal clime,
And dear the hearth-flame as the altar fire;
When fate accomplished wins her utmost bourne,
And fulness ousts for aye fair images,
Will doting mem'ry from their funeral pyre
Rise phoenix-wise and earth-sick spirits yearn
For fragrant flower, and sward, and changeful trees,
For storied rose, and sweet poetic morn,
For sound of bird, and brook, and murmuring bees,
For luckless fancies of illusion born,
What time in dark we dwelt and framed our lore?
Woe, woe, if then regretful we should mourn
"What wisdom left we on that human shore!"
For brooding kindness can a charm beget,

Not duly won, and from Heaven's parapet
These terrene colours shine with starry gleam—
But this is all a fable and a dream;
A fable, for this axiom it brings,
Immortal loves must love immortal things;
Dream is it, for uncurbed it took its flight,
And roamed afar, a fancy of the Night.

CHAPTER XIV.

The roses in the gardens of Lehna Singh hung their heads, the sunbeams danced no longer, and the pleasant fountains fell with monotonous plash on sullen pools, where goldfish hid themselves and sad swans floated apart. Moti wept in her bower, and Nature, which sympathizes with the good, grieved around her. The sun-birds flew away, for their gay plumage is not for times of mourning, but the doves lingered and hushed their wooing that they might not offend the disconsolate.

And this was Moti's garden, where happiness and beauty had once their dwelling.

Bloomy roses die,
Wan the petals floating,
Whirling on the breeze's sigh,
Ah, the worms were gloating,
This is by-and-bye.

In the great hall princes and nobles feasted with mirth and music. Laughter and outcries and mad revelry re-echoed through the stately archways and marble courts. Lal Singh was there, and great honour was rendered to him, for this was the time of his betrothal, and the bride was Moti. The festival had lasted for two days, and would be prolonged for many more. Moti was forgotten. The little maid who loved her lay on the floor at her feet and wept because Moti wept. Those who with zither and dance should have beguiled the hours, had stolen away to peep through latticed screens at the revelry.

Moti thought of Atmâ and moaned, but the little maid thought only of her mistress, and bewailed the fate that had joined her bright spirit by unseen bonds of love to one pre-doomed by inheritance to misfortune.

"For adversity loved his father's house," she sighed; "it is ill to
consort with the unfortunate, for in time we share their woe."
But Moti wrung her beautiful hands and cried:
"Ah if this breath of mine might purchase his!
Then death were fair and lovely as he said
In that enchanted even hour when he
Of love, and death, and moans, and constancy
Told till dark things grew lovely, and o'erhead
Sweet stars seemed ghosts, and shadow all that is.
But I have lost my life and yet not death

Have won, and now to me shall joy be strange,
And all my days the kindly winds that breathe
From mirthful groves of Paradise shall change
In my poor songless soul to wail, and sigh,
And moan, and hollow silence—let me die!
Poor me! who fearless snatched at bliss so high,
Witless! and yet to be of slight esteem
And little worth is sometimes well, no dream
Of high unrest, no awful afterglow
Affrights us simple ones when that we die.
Vain flickering lamps soon quenchéd—we but go
From this brief day, this short transition,
This interlude of farcial joy and woe,
Back to our native, kind oblivion.
Can this be Moti, she who prates of being,
And life, and death, and fallacy, and moan?
Ah, how should I be fixed and steadfast? seeing
All things about me shift, I need must change;
Things which I thought were plain are waxen strange,
Things are unfathomable which I deemed

Atmâ

Shallow and bare; nay, maid, I do not rave,
Sunbeams are mysteries, and Love that seemed
All wingéd joy, and transport light as air,
Ah me, but Love is deeper than the grave,
Is deeper than the grave; I seek it there.
Dear Death, bind Love for me, till that I die!
And he is doomed to die who loved me!

O bitter, bitter end of tenderness!
O doleful issue of my happiness!
Weep, little maid, for one that loved me!
O might I with my last of mortal breath
Bid him the cruel treachery to flee,
And hear his voice and sink to happy death,
So still might live the one that lovéd me!
Cease, kindly maid, arise, and whisper low,
As moon to weeping clouds, until there rise
Like pallid rainbow, wan with spectral glow,
A thing of fearful joy athwart my skies,
A hope, a joy e'en yet that this might be,
That I should die for him who lovéd me.
I waste no life, no blame shall me dismay,
For these brief days of mine are but a morn,
A handful of poor violets, wind-worn,
Or nurseling lily-buds which to mislay
Were not the ill that to the perfect flower
Might be if cruel hand should disarray
Its starry splendour when in ripened hour
It floats in tranquil state on Gunga's stream.
Make ready, little maid; sweet is the gleam

That lightens this ill night, soft clouds will weep,
The fervid bulbul still his song, beneath
Our tallices the blinking jasmines sleep,
The kindly myrtles shadow all our parth.
Speak, gentle maid, tell me it shall be so,
That I shall find my love; speak and we go
On pilgrimage more sweet than home-bent wing
Of banished doves—now, I will chant of woe,
And though my song be doleful, blithe I sing."
O Night!
O Night so true!
The promise of the Day is full of guile.
Fair is the Day, but crafty is her smile;
The friendly Night, it knows no subtle wile.
Dear Night!
Bring weeping dew,
And sad enchantments to undo the spells
Of baleful day, while from thy silent cells
Of dusk and slumber, still heart's-peace exhales.
O Night!
O Night, pursue
The bitter Day, and from her keeping wrest
Those cruel spoils, and to my empty breast
Give lethean calm, and dearest death, and rest.

CHAPTER XV.

The Rajah of Kashmir and his court went a-hunting on the day of Lal Singh's return to their good company. They swept down the valley, a gorgeous train of nobles and host of attendants with falcons girt for foray, and moved with much state and circumstance among the hills until the sun grew hot, when silken tents were pitched in a walnut grove near by a smoothly flowing river. Here they ate and drank and reposed while obsequious servants fanned them, and the sweet music of vinas blended with the murmur of the water and the droning of the bees.

The Rajah sat in the entrance of a crimson tent and enjoyed the delicious air. The nest-laden branches drooped above, the twittering of birds ceased, but gentle forms hopped lightly from twig to twig, and curious eyes peeped from leafy lurking-places. In the turban of the Rajah, the Sapphire of Fate shone with serene lustre like the blue water-lily of Kashmir. His fingers toyed idly with the plumage of a magnificent hawk, now unhooded but still wearing the leathern jesses and tiny tinkling bells of the chase. The leash by which it was held slipped gradually from the arm of an attendant and it was unconfined. Its keen eye knew all the ambushed flurry overhead, but it did not rise—a more curious prey lay nearer.

In a moment it was poised in air. Another second and it had gained possession of the Mystic Stone, the augur of weal to the Khalsa, its menace when borne by a foe, the portentous Sapphire of Fate!

All was consternation and clamour. The unlucky fellow who had slipped the leash, waving his wrist, sought to induce the bold robber to alight, but his cries were scarcely heard above the vociferation of the throng, and he was fain to tear his beard and curse the day of his birth. But as neither lamentation nor rage could restore the treasure, cooler heads dispatched a party of horsemen with falcons and lures to decoy the recreant.

With the first shout of dismay and horror Atmâ stood as if transfixed, enwrapt in thought, and did not stir nor speak until the rescuing party had long vanished across the plain, and Bertram touching him on the shoulder rallied him on his abstraction, and told him that the Nawab was about to beguile the time and reanimate the flagging spirits of the illustrious company with a tale. Repressing a sigh, Atmâ smiled and suffered his friend to lead him into the circle forming about the story-teller.

"Far back," began the Nawab, "far back in the ages whose annals are lost in story, when, Time and Eternity being nearer the point of their divergence, things preternatural and strange entered into the lives of men, there lived a mighty king of great renown, who, being stricken with a lingering but fatal malady, spent the last years of his life in adjusting the affairs of his kingdom and preparing all things to the single end that the reign of his successor, who was his only son, might excel in grandeur and dominion all other empires of that era. This son ascended the throne while still of tender years, and found that parental fondness had endowed him with unequalled power and dominion. His subjects, under the beneficent rule of the departed king, had become a great and prosperous nation; he was at peace with all neighbouring monarchs; his treasuries were filled to overflowing; and, more than all, the wisdom of the counsellors whom the king this father had appointed to instruct and guide his early years had sunk deep into a heart well-fitted by Nature to receive it, and his demeanour was such that the loyal affection which was his by inheritance soon changed to a heartfelt admiration and love of the virtues which all men perceived him to possess. Surely no monarch ever began to reign under more auspicious skies. One of his palaces, his chief pleasure-house, had been built for him by command of the late king, and was of unique excellence. Its progress during erection had been impatiently watched by the monarch, who desired to see it complete and be assured of its perfection before he closed his eyes on the world, so that the skilful builders who wrought day and night were distracted between the injunction laid on them that it should be in every part of unrivalled beauty, and the hourly repetition of the royal mandate that the task be accomplished immediately. But, notwithstanding, so well did they succeed that among all the wonderful palaces of that age and land there was none to compare with The Magic Isle, for thus was it called, because by ingenious device it floated on the bosom of one of the lakes by which that country was diversified. No bridge led to this palace, but gilded barges were ever ready to spread their silken sails and convey the king to and from the elysium, which sometimes, as if in coquetry, receded at his approach among flower-decked islands, and sometimes bore down to meet the gay flotilla, branches spread and garlands waving, like some enchanted vessel of unknown fashion and fragrance.

"But strange to tell, the young king grew every day more grave and pensive in the midst of all these delights. Music nor mirth could win him from the melancholy which overshadowed him. The truth was, that amid so much adulation as surrounded him, the idol of a nation, his soul no longer increased in wisdom; and loving virtue beyond all other things, he secretly bemoaned his defection whilst not perceiving its cause. His virtues, the cynosure of all eyes, withered like tender flowers meant to blossom in the shade, but unnaturally exposed to noon-day. His adoring people bewailed what they thought must be a foreshadowing of mortal illness, and the wise counsellors of his childhood vainly strove to fathom his mood. But those who know us best are ever the Unseen, and about the young monarch hovered the benignant influences that had watched his infancy, and now rightly interpreted the sorrow of his heart. In sooth, that this sorrow was matter of rejoicing in the Air, I gather from the joyous mien of that river-sprite which one day surprised him as he languidly mused in a balcony that overhung the water, and spoke to him in accents strange to his ear and yet at once comprehended.

"'Come, O king, my voice obey;
Come where hidden things are seen;
Come with me from garish day,
Withering, blasting, grievous, vain,
To retreat of mystery,
Haunt of holy mystery.'

"These words, as I have related, were spoken in an unknown tongue, and yet my story gives the mystic speech in pleasant and familiar rhythm. I do not know how this may be," and Nawab Khan gravely shook his head, "but perchance in recounting his experience, the king, unable to exactly reproduce in his own tongue the message brought to him by the sprite, for the thoughts of the Immortals cannot be expressed in human speech, conveyed a semblance of it in such words as he could command, and sought to veil their incompetency by an agreeable measure. In like manner I think may the art of poetry have been invented. It is an effort to cover by wile of dulcet utterance the impotence of mortal speech to tell the things that belong to the spirit. And, after all, language as we know it is an uncertain interpreter of even human emotions. So many of our words, and they our dearest, are but symbols representing unknown quantities.

"But to return to my story," continued the Nawab, "the sprite waving her arms beckoned the king to follow her, and led the way towards the river's mouth. It entered the lake only a short distance from where they were. The king experienced a poignant grief when for a moment he feared that, unable to follow her, he must forever lose sight of his beauteous visitant. But in another instant he was stepping into a tiny skiff which suddenly appeared where a moment before had floated a lily. The magical craft followed its spirit guide, moving against the tide, impelled by unseen power, and ever and anon the sprite beckoned him onward. Soon they entered the river, which here was deep, broad, and smoothly flowing. Motion ceased when they were under a high overhanging bank whose drooping foliage screened them from view. Here his guide again spoke:

"'Ask and ye hear, O king, 'tis meet
That mortal want should be replete
From fulness of immortal state.'

"At once his soul's sadness found voice and he cried:

"'Tell me how may my increase in virtue resemble this river in its onward flow?'

"Then the spirit answered:

"'From veiled spring that river sweeps
Whose swelling tides in glory
Roll onward to th' infinite deeps,
It is the soul's own story.'

"Again she beckoned him on, and without effort of his own he glided over the water until they paused again where a lotus flower rested on the tide. The bees clustered around it, attesting its sweetness, and when the king bent over it and breathed its odour he cried:

"'Ah, how shall my piety be pure like the lotus, and the savour of my virtues spread abroad?'

"And again the sprite replied:

"'Fairest flowers bloom unseen,
Graces that are manifest
Are of largess less serene;

Ever veiléd things are best.'

"When the eve deepened they were in a forest, a single star overhead shone through the gloom, and was reflected in the water. Looking upward the king asked for the third time:

"'How shall the days of my life be glorious and shine like the stars?'

"Ere she plunged beneath the flood to vanish forever, his guide answered:

"'Love, like the star, the shade of eve,
Seclusion, heavenly rest,
And calm, for these things interweave
The bowers of the Blest?'

"The king was now at the river's secret source, and on the bank above the deep pool he saw a man of a more princely aspect than any he had ever known. He stood grand and divine, extending his hand with a most benignant smile, and the story goes that the king perceived that he held a luminous gem, some say a diamond and some an emerald—both stones, as has often been proved, having magical potency. I cannot tell what it was, but the king reached out his own hand to touch it, when instantly, he knew not how, it seemed that something, a Resolve, a Desire, who can say what, went from him into the bright orb, bearing which the creature of light arose through the air, ascending higher and higher, bearing the jewel which shone like the everlasting stars. And the king knew that his soul's life had gone to other regions beyond the knowledge and speech of men.

"The magical skiff bore him swiftly down the stream and disappeared as he stepped from it to his palace. And tradition has it that his heaviness of heart was gone from that night, and that his soul increased in excellence and beauty, but that of its hidden life he was ever averse to tell."

CHAPTER XVI.

When the Nawab had concluded his tale, much discourse ensued regarding the unusual occurrences he had related and their significance.

"And," said the Rajah, who was a lover of verse, "how true it is that poetry lends an illusive charm to conceptions ordinary in themselves, like a lovely screen which bestows a grace on the scantiness it only half conceals. Poetry hath an advantage over prose."

"But an advantage compensated on the other hand by the elusiveness of its lightsome spirit, its grace so easily lost," said a poet who wrote songs for the pleasure of the Court. "The charm of poetry," he said sadly, "is too ethereal to live in sordid company, and perishes oft in the handling that had only proved the vigour of prose."

It is a primary characteristic of poetry that it cannot be translated. The most that a translator can do is to express in another tongue the main thought embodied, and enshrine it in a new poem. I have in changing some dainty wind-blossom of song from one dialect to another of the same language witnessed its instant transition into the realms of prose, and regarded the metamorphosis with the guilty awe of one who deals unwittingly in baleful magic.

And now they spoke of the marvellous properties of precious stones, a topic suggested, no doubt, by the story-teller's mention of a gleaming jewel, and probably still more by the unspoken anxiety with which many noted the non-return of the party who had gone in quest of the Sapphire.

"The diamond is possessed of many occult powers," said a courtier.

"Ay," replied another, "among gems the diamond has greater subtlety than all others."

"I would like," said one, "to wear a circlet of well-chosen stones to serve as oracle and counsellor. The opal should assure me of my friend's fealty, the invisible slaves of the diamond should guard my fortunes, the serpent that cast its harmful eye on me would be blinded by my emerald, for, in fine, I believe that vassal genii attend each gem, and obey the behests of him who holds it."

"The diamond," said the poet, "guards the destinies of lovers."

"Love," said Atmâ smiling, "is its own security, for it makes no unwilling captive."

The look of hatred and rage which Lal Singh darted at him startled the onlookers.

"The worst of sorcerers," said he, "are those who disclaim the use of enchantment. Success in love, Atmâ Singh, means sometimes to die like a dog."

But the Nawab interposed with moderate speech. "It is," said he, "a wise man who knows the omens of the future, and is thereby guided."

"The services of a skilful necromancer are greatly needed at the present," whispered a courtier.

Many of the company were now standing, scanning with anxious gaze the distant horizon. They looked far a-field, but high overhead the robber looked down on them. There was the falcon mid-way between earth and sky. Now it began to sink. Swiftly it fell, and a cry escaped the lips of the few who observed it. The bird's keeper was off with the expedition, but as it reached the earth, a very few yards from the Rajah's circle, a dozen men were instantly upon it. Foremost was Atmâ Singh, his hand it was that grasped it. It was tired, and stood on his left wrist with anything but the air of a convicted thief, as with head bent sideways it inspected the throng.

Atmâ strode forward to the Rajah, and a dismayed cry arose that the Sapphire was lost indeed. The bird no longer held it. Atmâ took no heed, but advancing made obeisance before Golab Singh, and extended to him his captive.

"Your clemency, Maharajah," he said, "for the truant."

"Had he brought back the Sapphire he might have gained mercy," said the Rajah, with more anger, Bertram thought, than he had ever seen him display. "Take away the knave out of my sight, and despatch a horseman at once to the Palace with command that four hundred men forthwith search all this plain, with every tree on it and every stream that crosses it, until they find the jewel."

Lal Singh since his angry outburst had stood aside, his narrow face contracted, and had not ceased to watch Atmâ from the moment when he seized the falcon. His cunning eyes followed the young Sikh as he bowed before the Ruler of Kashmir, and now gliding forward he cringed before Golab Singh, as he hissed in a voice nearly inarticulate with triumph and hate, "Maharajah, the plain is wide; before entering on so extensive an undertaking, order someone more trusty than Atmâ Singh to recover the stone by searching the leal descendant of the holy Nanak! I, though less lofty of sentiment and aspiration, am filled with horror and grief, because I have perceived him to take the Sapphire from the bird the moment it touched ground."

The effect of this charge can hardly be described: indignation on the part of some, among whom were Atmâ's British friends, at what they felt assured must be a groundless accusation; suspicion and anger on the part of others. "Let him immediately be seized and searched," commanded the Rajah.

The first part of his command was already obeyed, and almost before a protest could be uttered, Atmâ's arms were bound behind him and Golab Singh's servants proceeded zealously to search his person. In silence and with lips compressed, Bertram and his brother officers looked on whilst he submitted to this indignity, no syllable escaping him from the moment when he fixed his accusing gaze on his foe. But when a tiny onyx-box of curious workmanship was produced from the folds of his girdle, and laid before the Rajah of Kashmir, he did not repeat the look, although on its appearance Lal uttered an exulting exclamation.

The onyx-box was all that rewarded the scrutiny of the Rajah's servants. "Open it!" he commanded, and forthwith the fatal casket was unclosed. Golab Singh, bending over it, inhaled the strong and subtle odour that had nearly overcome Atmâ the morning he received the box from the hands of Nama at the sacred shrine. The Maharajah turned pale, and with difficulty recovered his breath. "Miscreant!" cried the courtiers.

Now a paper was unfolded bearing the seal and superscription of the Maharanee Junda Kowr, the dangerous foe of the British to whom Golab Singh owed his throne.

"An emissary of the Ranee," cried some.

"A spy," shouted others, while Golab Singh had thoughts which it would not have been prudent to utter aloud in that mixed assemblage.

"A despatch from the Ranee withheld by this traitor for who knows what villainous purpose!"

"He shall pay the penalty," he thundered, "before the sun rise to-morrow. Carry him bound to a dungeon!"

Now an Englishman who stood beside him touched the prisoner on the shoulder. His face had grown stern, and he narrowly searched Atmâ's countenance as he spoke gravely but gently enough. "Have you no word to say, Atmâ Singh, when you are accused of playing so base a conspirator's part against the life of your host and of your friends?"

Then Atmâ spoke and proudly, "No word, Sahib, which a Sikh may utter."

Excitement prevailed and great consternation. Englishmen exchanged glances; plots, they believed, of an unguessed extent surrounded them. Musselmen and Sikhs looked at one another with fierce suspicion. "Where," their faces asked, "are his accomplices?" And no look of doubt fell on his denouncer. The Rajah's rage increased every moment, adding to the commotion which delayed the fulfilment of his commands. To enhance the confusion, the party of horsemen now returned. They pressed around, hearing and giving tidings. In the tumult Bertram reached Atmâ's side, but before he could speak, Atmâ whispered in his ear, "Meet me in the Muslim Burying ground to-morrow night." Then with a sudden and strong effort, swift as a bird, he freed himself from the excited uncertain grasp that held him, and springing upon a horse he was off on the wings of the wind. A score of men scrambled to their saddles, but they were in confusion, and their horses were tired, whilst Atmâ had mounted a fresh horse just brought forward for his own safe escort to prison. In the disorder, he gained a few priceless moments of time, and threading well his way between the groves that dotted the plain, he was soon lost to view.

Caroline Augusta Frazer

CHAPTER XVII.

How fair is Night, how hushed the scene,
Earth's teeming hosts are here no longer seen,
Only a chosen few,
A happy few,
The blooming cereus and the blessed dew
Ordained have been
To weave beneath the solemn moon and still,
Some holy rite, some mystic pledge fulfil.
That loveliest star fades from my sight,
Leaves the fond presence of the doting night,
And softly sinks awhile,
A little while,
Its radiance into brief exile
From mourning night.
So shall my blissful flame of life expire,
So fail from light, and love, and life's desire.

So pondered Atmâ in that strange calm that follows an overwhelming stroke of calamity. It was midnight, and the moon shone on the old Muslim Burial Place, where he awaited the coming of Bertram. The trees cast long black shadows, and here and there the monuments gleamed like silver. His mind had not yet grasped the full enormity of the conspiracy of which he was the victim, but he knew that the perfidy of Lal and the loss of the Sapphire meant death to his hopes of winning victory for the Khalsa. But his heart was strangely still. He had been waiting since sundown, but he did not doubt his friend, and interrupted his meditations every now and then to look expectantly in the direction whence he knew he must come. At length a figure emerged from the darkness and silence at the further end of a long avenue leading from the entrance, and Atmâ knew the form and step grown in those past days of pleasant intercourse so dear and familiar. He went to meet his friend; Bertram's face was graver than he had known it in the past, and the kindly eyes were full of questioning.

Atmâ spoke first, and the joyful tone of his voice surprised himself. Perhaps he was more hopeful at heart than he knew.

"My heart was assured that you would come, Bertram Sahib."

"My English friends," replied Bertram, "have left Jummoo, and are now on their way to Lahore, where I must join them. I could not go without an effort to meet you here, not only because you bade me, but I also desired it, for I have been full of distressful perplexity, refusing to doubt you, my friend whom I have believed leal and true."

"But you are grieved no longer," returned Atmâ. "As your eyes meet mine, their sadness vanishes like the clouds of morning before the light of day."

Bertram smiled. "True, the candour of your ingenuous gaze does much to reassure me. I gather from your brief reply to my brother officer that loyalty to your nation and faith forbids you to speak openly, but surely this much you can tell me, for I ask concerning yourself alone:—Can it be that you who have seemed an embodiment of truth and candour have all this time been contemplating the destruction of your host, and my destruction also," he added slowly, "whose hand has so often been clasped in yours? Truth and Purity seemed dear to you, Atmâ Singh. Can it be possible that you and I have together searched into heavenly truth, while one of us held in his heart the foulest treachery?"

"I know of no treachery to Golab Singh," replied Atmâ steadfastly. "As for you, brother of my love, reflect that the dear hope, faint and distant though it be now, of the triumph of the Khalsa need not imply disgrace nor disaster to your people, who, unwillingly at first, burdened themselves with the affairs of the Punjaub. The later treachery at Mooltan has been abundantly expiated by the innocent as well as the guilty."

He stopped abruptly, for a sound like distant sobbing broke the stillness. They listened, but it was not repeated.

"Atmâ, I believe you. I can perceive your position, and how, so unhappily, you have been able to reconcile insidious intrigue with sentiments of honour and purity. But I have much to tell you, for I would warn you against enemies on all sides. Rajah Lal, for some reason your mortal foe, has convinced Golab Singh that you connived at his death by means of the poison discovered in the casket." Here the Englishman's eyes sought Atmâ's with sorrowful question in their blue depths, but he received no other response than a frank and fearless gaze. "He accuses you," continued Bertram, "of conspiring to rob him, Lal Singh, of his bride," Atmâ started, "for it seems his betrothal was celebrated during his recent absence from Kashmir. But I have startled you, Atmâ Singh, tell me—"

A woman's scream interrupted him. It sounded near by, and both sprang forward, when Bertram, recollecting himself, stayed his companion.

"Halt," he said, "you must remain concealed. I will go alone if we hear more."

Another shriek rent the air, and he hastened forward, Atmâ proceeding slowly in the same direction by a more circuitous way. He was stunned by what he had just heard. It seemed to him that the shriek which had broken into the midst of Bertram's communication had been his own, and that it was being repeated on all sides. In reality the only sound that now disturbed the night was the echo of his own and Bertram's footsteps, the latter hurried and irregular for the ground was uneven.

A few moments passed and the steps ceased, and Atmâ standing still heard a smothered exclamation. Another voice spoke from a distance angrily, and, fearing for his friend, he now hastened forward rapidly, though still cautiously. When he reached the spot, he found Bertram kneeling beside a prostrate female form, a small and childlike figure. The veil, torn aside, was stained with blood, and Atmâ's heart stood still, for the unconscious form was that of Moti's little maid. He failed to see Bertram's imperative gesture, motioning him back, and Bertram then spoke in rapid though subdued accents.

"Go back, I entreat you; no one will harm me, but your life is marked—"

He had better not have spoken. There was a cry of fiendish glee and then the report of a gun, and Bertram fell back with a groan. A shriek of triumph rose at a distance. "The traitor Atmâ is dead!" A noise of the flying feet of Lal's minions and then silence. Atmâ stood alone. With anguished heart he raised the unconscious head which his own love had lured to destruction. To his unspeakable joy the eyes opened, and the loved voice faintly strove to bid him fly. The effort made him swoon again, and when he next revived it was to ask for water. Atmâ ran to a rill which he had noted before, and speedily returned with a draught. After drinking, Bertram raised himself slightly, and directing his friend's attention to the body of the servant-maid he whispered:

"With her last breath she bade me search the tomb." Until now Atmâ had not observed that they were in the shadow of Sangita's tomb. The vines were torn from its ancient portal, which hung open on broken hinge.

"Go," said Bertram, but Atmâ would first staunch and bind his wound.

At length he might leave him, and then lifting the door and the trailing vines aside to allow the moonlight to penetrate he looked in. A moment later he had entered. He remained long, so long that Bertram, uneasy and suffering, called him again and again, but without response. Half an hour—an hour passed, and then he feebly and painfully crept to the doorway of the tomb. He saw Atmâ prostrate on the damp sepulchral mould, his face buried in his hands, and beside him lay still, and cold, and lifeless, a girl attired in bridal finery, with jewels gleaming on her dark hair and on her stiffening arms. It was Moti.

Ah, the worms were gloating,

This is by-and-bye.

Caroline Augusta Frazer

CHAPTER XVIII.

Far retired in the woody recesses to the south of Jummoo, thither come by a winding labyrinth of ways were the fugitives. Bertram, languid and pale, lay on a couch of moss and leaves built by his friend. His gaze rested on Atmâ with compassion, for he knew that his wound was of the spirit, and he feared that without a balm the sore must be mortal. The soul dies sometimes before we say of the man "he is dead," and at that strange death we shudder lest it should know no awakening.

Atmâ sat near by, dumb and unheeding. His fingers toyed idly with a Pearl, on which he gazed as if seeing other forms than those about him. For many hours he was silent, rising at times to proffer food and water to the wounded man, but oblivious of his own needs, and only half-conscious that he was not alone. Daylight faded and stars came out before he spoke, addressing none and looking away into silence:—

"O swift-winged Time,
Bearing to what unknown estate,
What silent clime,
The burden of our hopes and fears,
The story of our smiles and tears,
And hapless fate?
Those vanished days,
Their golden light can none restore;
Those sovereign rays
That set o'er western seas to-night,
This tranquil moon that shines so bright,
Have paled before
Returning in their time, but, oh!
The golden light of long ago

Returns no more.
This little Pearl,
Of water born, shall year by year
Imprison in its tiny sphere
Those fleeting tints whose mystic strife
And shadowy whirl
Of colour seem a form of life;
Nor ever shall their sea-born home
Dissolve in foam;
But this frail build of love and trust
Will sink to dust."

The magnitude of his calamity had dulled the sharpness of each stroke, and thus it was not of loss of love, faith and fortune that he spoke, but of the frailty of life. This is our habit. A ship too richly freighted goes down, and straightway the owner laments, not his own deprivation, but that "all flesh is grass." "Vanity of vanities," he cries, "all is vanity," and we but guess at his hurt. A mysterious consciousness is wiser than his reason, and connects the broken current of his life with a mighty movement which he knows afar, but cannot tell whether it be of Time or Eternity. He who designed all, "did not He make one?"

Our days are empty, how should they be otherwise in a world whose very vanity is infinite?

"Imperial Sorrow loves her sway, or I had sooner broken your vigil, my brother," said Bertram. "I perceive that the falsity of life appals your spirit. It is true that the faint lustre of that tiny orb will long survive these poor frames of ours; it is a fitting emblem of the deathless tenant within."

But to Atmâ it was the symbol of a lost love. He looked on it listlessly. It seemed a long while since Moti died, for in his heart joy, and hope, and youth had died since. The immortal destiny of man, a belief dear to the Sikh, seemed a thing indifferent. Death might not be final, but it was yesterday he mourned, and of it he said: "it is past."

He knew of the soul's Immortality, but of the Continuity of Life he had not heard,

Dear Life, cling close, true friend, thro' well or ill,
Mine aye, we cannot part our company.
Though breathing cease and busy heart be still,
Together will we wake eternally.
Strange Life, in whose immeasurable clasp,
The past, the present and the vast to be
Mingle,—O Time, the world is for thy grasp,
I and my life for immortality.
Those bygone hours that were too bright to stay,
And vanished from my sight like morning mist,
Will dawn again, and, ne'er to fade away,
The fleeting moments endlessly exist.
The present lives, the past and future twine;
My life, my days forevermore endure.
My life—it comes I know not whence, but mine
For aye 'twill be, indissolubly sure.

When the night drew on, Atmâ went away. In thought Bertram followed him, full of sad solicitude.

He strode along the heights. The cooling air and the sense of isolation were grateful to his worn spirit. He wandered far until he found himself in a rocky fortress, vast, black and terrible. The lowering peaks above inclined their giant heads to one another in awful conclave, and the ghastly moonbeams pierced to the gloom below, where they enwrapped the lonely form of Atmâ in a phosphorescent glare. The winds broke among the cliffs, and with shrieks and fearful laughter proclaimed the dark councils of the peaks, and in the din were heard mutterings and imprecations. A transport seized the soul of Atmâ. The horrible glee of the night awoke wrath, and he hurled defiance to the mocking winds.

"What! are th' infernal powers moved for me,
That all the hosts of hell me welcome give,
And claim me comrade in their revelry?
Abhorrent things, I am not yours, I live,
I know I live because I think on death!
I live, dead things, to revel among tombs,
A ghoul, henceforth I feast on buried joys,
My soul the burial-place, where lie, beneath
A fearful night of cries and hellish spumes,
My lovely youth with jovial convoys,
Hopes, happy-eyed, and linked solaces,
And in the lapse of hateful years they will—
My guileless joys, my rose-hued memories—
Corrupt and rot and turn to venomed ill.
O cherished dreams of Truth! O sacred bond
Unlovely grown! O faith so mutable!
Shades of my fathers, not august but fond!
How hollow were the darlings of my dream!
But she, O Lotus-flower, my promised bride,
Star of my youth, my pure unspotted dove!
Again I see her in her gentle pride,
Her starry eyes meet mine with melting beam;
Unsightly grief approach not near my Love,
Flee from her presence, O thou gaunt Despair,
Good Time, embalm her daintily and fair,
Link her sweet fame with hymns and fragrancy.
And happy stars, and blissful utterance,
And with all transports that immortal be.

Atmâ

Fold her, good Time, from my remembrance,
O, this is bitterest mortality,
That living heart of love should be the urn
Where lie the ashes of our joys that turn
To bitterness, and all our lives o'erflow
Till dearest love be grown a hateful woe;
My sun of youth has set, methinks it should
Have set with such a splendour as had all
My sober days with mellow light imbued;
O bitter sun of youth whose knavish pledge
Of high-born hope and holy privilege
But led me undefended to my fall,
O lamentable day when I was born!
What shapes are those that mock me with their scorn?
What trumpet-call is this within my breast?
I am grown wise, my senses are increased,
It is the breath of fiends that drowns my speech,
The bellowing of devils as they feast.
I am the taunt of devils, and they preach
Of death, of cursing, and of endless woe;
The lightnings of this devil-tempest show
Horrors not dreamed of
O thou Vengeful Power,
I am forspent, if merit there can be
In self accusing, in this darkest hour
O hear me, and I pray thee pity me,
For I have sinned, O fool, unwise and blind!
 And I am Atmâ; whom thou hadst designed
For life of sanctity and holy quest.
Lord, I am Atmâ, and I have transgressed;
I sought the Present whom we may not seek,

The Future whom I slighted went before
And waited arméd and my goods did take.
This is my sin that sent on high behest
I slept; Lord, as one waited at thy golden door
A hundred years, and snatched a little rest,
And waked to see the closing gateway drawn
And lived thereafter only in the dawn
Of that brief moment's light, so also I
Must dream of wasted radiance till I die."

CHAPTER XIX.

The quiet days were passing slowly. Bertram's wound did not heal, and his strength grew less. The unseen powers that throng the air and watch our ways arranged about him the phantasmagoria of dissolution. It was the waning of the moon. A tender mist, which had long veiled a mountain crest, now unfolded its depths and was wafted away. A star shot across the welkin and was no more seen. Summer blossoms faded with the dying season. The music of the pine-boughs had a more melancholy cadence, and birds of passage took their flight. Atmâ marked these things, and often withdrew to lament.

One evening they watched the shadows lengthening. Atmâ's heart was oppressed, but Bertram looked on the shifting scene with happy undaunted smile. In voice pathetic only from mortal weakness and strong with immortality he said:

"When mists and dreams and shadows flee,
And happy hills so far and high
Bend low in benedicite,
I know the break of day is nigh.
Thus have I watched in daisied mead
A grayer heaven bending low,
And heard the music of a brook
In meet response more softly flow,
Until at mystic signal given
From realm entranced the spell was riven,
The sunbeams glanced,
The wavelets danced,
And gladness spread from earth to heaven.
This little flower
Right bravely blooming at my feet

So dainty, sweet,
Has missed the spirit of the hour.
But stay, the tender calyx thrills,
It feels the silence of the hills,
Behold it droops, in haste to be
At one with that hushed company."
Atmâ:
"Not day, but night, beloved friend,
Long doleful night,
The shadows of the eve portend."
Bertram:
"Watcher unseeing! what of the night!
'Tis past and gone.
I know th' advance and joy of light!
Look how for it all things put on
Such hues as in comparison
The earth and sky to darkness turn,
Hues of the sard, and chrysolite
And sapphire herald in the morn."
Atmâ:
"Ah! woe is me for day so quickly past,
For morning fled, and noontide unexpressed."
Bertram:
"The subtly-quickening breath of morn
my inmost being is borne,
And I behold th' unearthly train
Of solemn splendours that pertain
To seraph state,
Such as our glories symbolize.
They sweep in countless bright convoys
Athwart my blissful view, they seem

Completion of all pleasure known
Or loved, and of our fairest dream
End and interpretation."
Atmâ:
"Let be, my friend; so it be morn to thee
I make no moan, though thy day's dawn shall be
Night of desertion and lament to me."

Caroline Augusta Frazer

CHAPTER XX.

Death, whether it be day or night, overtook Bertram in the mountain fastness, and Atmâ knew once more that the human soul is lonely, which he had been fain to doubt or deny in the pleasant delusion of friendship. He lived alone, and, after a while, with returning mental health, he sometimes gave way to bitter reflection on these, his wasted days, though knowing himself unable still to take up the broken thread of active existence. But, growing stronger, he was at last able to perceive that this apparently barren season was the best harvest time of his life, for, adrift from human ties and from religions, he was at last alone with God. His battles were sore to fight, the solid earth seemed gone from beneath his feet, and the heavens were become an illusion. There was a time when he cried out that "all men are liars," as we have all cried, but the instinct of the soul happily arrested him then. Happily, for it is strangely true that he who loses faith in man will soon lose faith in God. It is as if the great heart of the Racé, recoiling from suicidal impulse, warned the individual from treason against his kind—a suggestion of the unity underlying all created things. This the best religions have known, and have founded on it a law that he who loves God must love his brother also. Apprehending this, Atmâ grew again in heart to forgive his fellowmen who had so sorely sinned against him, and, musing on their ways he pitied them, and knew that the true attitude towards humanity is one of pity. He pitied men in their crimes, in their unbeliefs, and in their faiths, and presently he saw in these faiths which he had decried a spiritual beauty. His own creed, grown hateful to him as the vainest of delusions, reasserted its claims to reverence, and the voice that had cried to his childhood out of the desert of silence and mystery that surrounds every human soul spoke to him again as a voice of inspiration. Every man's faith is the faith of his fathers, the faith learned on his mother's knee. He, who, increasing knowledge, discerns the different degrees of darkness that characterize our religious theories, and chooses for himself one from among them, increases his soul's sorrow, for our light is darkness, and God is not to be found for searching. "It is not by our feet or change of place that men leave Thee nor return unto Thee." The quietness of habit is more conducive to spirituality than the progress whose gain is so infinitesimal, and whose heavy price is the destruction of the habit of faith. It is better to believe a falsehood than to doubt a truth. The habitual attitude of the soul, its upward gaze is more important than the quality of the veil through which it discerns the Eternal. During the days when Atmâ lived without the religion which was so mortal that it died in his heart because he found that its friends were false, he knew God, for this veil was removed, and when the weakness of human nature again demanded the support of habit and formula, he turned to the mystic rites and prayers endeared and hallowed by association, but he knew now that God is a spirit, for spirit with spirit had met. A silence, born of great reverence, rested upon him, and he no more clamoured to save the world. The fall of the Khalsa no longer meant the downfall of God, and in time even the heartache for the vanquishment of his early dreams disappeared.

And the memory of his love? Love is transient, but frozen lips and closed eyes can speak with a power unknown to the living, and the power abides to a longer day than the living voice had controlled. And so the night of his mourning was long, but the longest night has a dawn, and it seems to me that the saddest thing I can say in ending my tale is that the morning dawned and grief was forgotten. It is sad that we forget joys; it is sadder to forget sorrows.

And so this story of religion that called itself heavenly, and love that was most mortal, is over. Atmâ had had of earth's most beautiful things,

"O Love, Religion, Music—all
That's left of Eden upon earth,"—
but no—Love and Religion are not left.

THE END.

www.ingramcontent.com/pod-product-compliance
Lightning Source LLC
Chambersburg PA
CBHW020912080526
44589CB00011B/559